MAGDALENE'S LOST LEGACY

Symbolic Numbers and the Sacred Union in Christianity

MARGARET STARBIRD

Bear & Company
Rochester, Vermont

Bear & Company
One Park Street
Rochester, Vermont 05767
www.InnerTraditions.com

Bear & Company is a division of Inner Traditions International

Library of Congress Cataloging-in-Publication Data

Starbird, Margaret, 1942-
  Magdalene's lost legacy : symbolic numbers and the sacred union in
Christianity / Margaret Starbird.
      p. cm.
Includes bibliographical references and index.
  ISBN 1-59143-012-7 (pbk.)
  1. Mary Magdalene, Saint—Miscellanea. 2. Jesus Christ—
Miscellanea.
3. Bible. N.T.—Criticism, interpretation, etc.—Miscellanea. 4.
Gematria. I. Title.

  BS2485.S685 2003
  232.9—dc21
                                          2003004455

Printed and bound in the United States at Lakebook Manufacturing

10 9 8 7 6 5 4 3 2 1

Text design and layout by Virginia Scott Bowman
This book was typeset in Veljovic with Trajan and
Lucida Sans as the display typefaces

MAGDALENE'S
LOST
LEGACY

CONTENTS

IN SEARCH OF
THE LOST BRIDE

In August 1998 when I received the galleys of my second book, *The Goddess in the Gospels,* I was astonished to discover that the date appearing on each page of the final printout was 22 July, the designated feast day of Mary Magdalene. But this coincidence was minor compared to the powerful emotion I felt several days later when I finished editing the text and noticed, almost accidentally, that the number printed at the top of the last page of the final chapter was 153. For me this was a moment of profound synchronicity, for 153 is the symbolic number of the Mary called "the Magdalene"—the sum of the numerical values of the letters of the her Greek epithet η Μαγδαληνη found in the canonical Gospels. And because *The Goddess in the Gospels* was centered on the search for the original role and true importance of Mary Magdalene in the early Christian community, the pages printed on her feast day and the final page of text bearing her number seemed a confirmation of the quest I had undertaken. I felt I had not walked alone.

Readers of my earlier books have asked me to delve deeper into some of the themes addressed in those books: the search for the lost bride of Jesus and the archetype of the sacred union that was originally an important tenet of Christianity, but sadly lost in its later development. In part, the present volume is a response to those requests.

But an even stronger impulse for this book is my commitment to promoting a wider understanding of what I consider the original Christian mythology and doctrines that are present—in plain sight!—in the symbolic numbers found in the New Testament. Because of renewed appreciation for the sacred numbers codified by Greek philosophers and Hebrew Kabbalists in ancient times, readers will most certainly be interested in examining suppressed numerical codes discovered in the Gospels' passages and in the other canonical texts of Scripture commonly known as the Greek Bible.

In 1990 when I submitted the manuscript of my first book, *The Woman with the Alabaster Jar*, the editors decided that a chapter dealing with the symbolic numbers encoded in the Apocalypse of John (the Book of Revelation) was not entirely related to the woman who, according to the Gospel narratives, had anointed Jesus with precious unguent of nard from her alabaster jar. In this book, that rejected chapter has become the cornerstone. That chapter reveals secret meaning embedded in certain prominent Greek phrases found in the New Testament.

The authors of the New Testament applied gematria—a literary device whereby the sums of certain phrases produce significant sacred numbers—to convey special concepts. The practice of assigning numerical values to words was apparently common in the ancient world. In Hebrew and in Greek there were no separate symbols to represent numbers. In each language, the letters of the alphabet stood for number values, so, inescapably, the values of letters forming each word could be added together to yield a sum called that word's gematria. Certain names, epithets, and phrases of Scripture, both Hebrew and Greek, were carefully constructed so that their gematria would be consistent with the sacred numbers of the classical cosmology—the "canon of sacred number" derived by the mathematicians of the ancient world. The practice of gematria is like setting lyrics to music; in the Bible and other texts significant phrases were carefully and deliberately set to numbers.

Although its existence is not widely known to students of Christian Scripture, the practice of gematria throws new light on the meaning of many passages found in the New Testament. In 1971 I first encountered this use of numbers to elucidate and enhance the meaning of certain phrases in *The City of Revelation* by John Michell, the well-known British esoteric scholar and philosopher. His discussion of the canon of number and proportion and the implications of gematria for Christianity have had a radical influence on my own interpretation of the New Testament writings for more than thirty years.

Although the practice of gematria has continued unbroken in Hebrew, and is still used today by Orthodox Jewish rabbis, the use of numbers in interpreting the meaning of Christianity's sacred texts was anathematized by Irenaeus and other prominent Church fathers in the second and third centuries, and with the suppression of the Gnostic heresies, the practice of any kind of "numbers theology" apparently ceased. As Christianity spread to Western Europe, the lingua franca became Latin rather than Koiné, the form of Greek spoken and written in the eastern Mediterranean in the Hellenistic and Roman periods. Near the end of the fourth century, Saint Jerome translated the Greek Scriptures into Latin, with the direct result that every trace of the gematria in the original Koiné was lost. Given modern tools for computation and cross-referencing, this long-neglected interpretive practice needs to be examined for the remarkable new light it throws upon the faith of the earliest Christians. It appears that the "orthodox" were in many cases the real heretics!

In *The Woman with the Alabaster Jar*, I took certain liberties in interpreting passages from the four canonical Gospels, occasionally allowing intuition and common sense to lead to conclusions that are at variance with traditional interpretation. Many of my interpretations were triggered by hidden meanings encoded in the texts and the gematria that unlocks them. In the present work I hope to show how applying gematria to biblical texts leads to new interpretations and questions regarding these texts. For example: What did the first-century Christian communities, those for which the Gospels were written, really believe about Jesus? Which of his teachings may have been distorted? How might certain passages of Scripture have been misinterpreted? And what role can this "new light" play in restoring the full integrity of certain original Christian tenets?

In their passionate pursuit of the historical Jesus of Nazareth scholars like John Dominic Crossan, Geza Vermes, and Neil Douglas-Klotz have shifted focus away from the strong influence of Hellenic culture and classical philosophy on the first several centuries of the Christian movement in order to stress the Jewish or "Aramaic" Jesus. Jesus of Nazareth, whose story is told in the canonical Gospels, was a charismatic Jewish teacher, but the resurrected Christ found in the New Testament writings has much in common with the Greek gods Apollo and Dionysus, as well as other sacrificed gods—Dumuzi, Tammuz, Osiris, and Ba'al—from even more ancient mythologies in the Near East.

In *The Goddess in the Gospels*, I presented substantial evidence for the existence of the lost bride of Jesus—the Mary whose epithet was "the Magdalene." With the help of gematria I provided evidence that this woman was the true counterpart of the Lord, his bride and his beloved. Seeing Mary as the Bride of Christ may have been one reason Gnostic Christians were chastised for their "numbers theology," for the raising of Mary Magdalene to preeminent status was inevitable in light of her powerful sacred number, 153, and its significant associations with the Sacred Feminine. The reader must judge the case for the sacred union of the "Christ couple" on the merits of a vast body of circumstantial evidence, including the disclosure of the sacred numbers associated with the archetypal partners, the Beloveds. The gematria in the Gospels reveals the pearl of great price hidden in the field—the mystery of the "reign of God" and the *hieros gamos*, or "sacred marriage" of opposite energies, at the heart of the Christian story—too long denied. It is time to welcome the partnership paradigm with its inherent gender equality to our communal psyche and to the fundamental institutions of our civilization, both secular and religious: family, church, and government.

Through the years of my quest, I have attempted to see Jesus through the eyes of his contemporaries, Jews of the first century, an oppressed community suffering under the heavy yoke of Rome, militantly theocratic and suspicious of their own religious leaders, the priestly cult of Sadducees who collaborated shamelessly with the Roman conquerors. Much of this material can be inferred from the Gospel texts, although it has generally been misunderstood or ignored in sermons from Christian pulpits. For example, crucifixion was an exclusively Roman punishment reserved for seditionist rebels and slaves. The Gospel clearly states that it was Roman soldiers who nailed Jesus to the cross at Golgotha, and yet for centuries Christians mistakenly blamed the Jews for crucifying Jesus. It is time to confront the fact that some of what we thought we knew about Jesus and his message needs now to be reexamined in light of modern biblical scholarship. What did Jesus really teach? What did Jesus really do?

I have a friend who had a dream. She dreamed of a long caravan of dromedaries, heavily loaded with large bundles and packages strapped to their backs, totally bogged down in the arid waste of the Sahara. The exhausted dromedaries could go no further. They had sunk to their knees under the scorching sun and were resigned to giving up their struggle. The frantic camel drivers were desperately trying to whip the dehydrated animals into continuing their journey, but the poor creatures were finished. The mission of the entire caravan was clearly doomed, floundering in the desert sands. Finally, in the dream, the caravan drivers threw up their hands in surrender, dropped their whips, and sank to the sand, prostrating themselves next to their dying camels.

At this point in her dream, my friend woke up in a cold sweat, suddenly and acutely aware that the caravan represented the plight of Christianity at the threshold of the third millennium. At the same time, she realized that there was an obvious solution to the dilemma! At some point, the drivers of the caravan must divest the beasts of their awkward burdens and then mount the camels and RIDE! In a clear case of life and death, the baggage and "trappings" are dispensable! The "sacred journey" is too important to be allowed to founder in the scorching sands of the desert.

In light of the worldview of the twenty-first century, we must make conscious decisions as to which doctrines and traditions are indispensable to our journey, which support our value system, which nourish our faith. The trappings that hinder us and cause us to founder helplessly, the traditions and doctrines that no longer "hold water," must now be discarded. We must unload them and leave them in the desert, choosing to continue unencumbered on our journey of life! Paramount among these, in my opinion, is the distorted tradition that the human, historical Jesus was a celibate god.

Our present situation echoes one that occurred in the first century in Israel, when the offering of animal sacrifices in the Temple of Jerusalem was no longer possible because the Temple had been destroyed. Animal sacrifices had to be set aside and new practices of ritual and worship created. Like pious Jews and early Christians of that time, we must again attempt to create new wineskins for a new vintage.

In hopes of contributing to this effort, I have returned to the foundations of the faith of our fathers, to see what can be discovered that might help restore the integrity of Christian doctrines. I have searched the cultural history of the ancient world and European civilization, religious texts, esoteric dissertations, art, literature, and other caches of wisdom in an urgent quest for truth.

Always astonishing is the continuous stream of religious consciousness that started as a tiny rivulet—like a trickle of melted snow on a mountain peak—and is now gathering momentum, cascading over falls and into pools, coursing its way to the sea. These waters—the living waters of wisdom and truth—are the life-giving gift of the Spirit. May we drink of them now and always!

The first man never finished comprehending Wisdom
nor will the last succeed in fathoming her.
For deeper than the sea are her thoughts;
her counsels than the great abyss.
Now I, like a rivulet from her stream
channeling the waters into a garden
said to myself
"I will water my plants,
my flower bed I will drench."
And suddenly this rivulet of mine became a river,
then this stream of mine, a sea.
Thus do I send my teachings forth,
shining like the dawn,
to become known afar off.
Thus do I pour out instruction like prophecy
and bestow it on generations to come.

SIRACH 24:26–30

1

THE BLUEPRINT OF
THE COSMIC TEMPLE

It is my conviction that Christianity at its inception included the celebration of the hieros gamos, the "sacred marriage" of opposites, a model incarnate in the archetypal bridegroom and his bride—Jesus Christ and the woman called "the Magdalene." This model of unity, tragically lost in the cradle of Christianity, is patterned on the fundamental blueprint for life on our planet, and manifested in the leadership role played by certain women in the community of Jesus' first followers. Following the crucifixion of the sacrificed bridegroom, the memory of the sacred partnership of masculine and feminine energies at the heart of his ministry was gradually suppressed, being supplanted by a cult of the resurrected Lord of Hosts, seated in glory at the right hand of his Father on a celestial throne in heaven and served by a hierarchy of chosen male associates and their heirs.

Sacred partnership was not invented in the first century. It was ritually celebrated in many regions of the Near East long before the advent of Christianity. In Mesopotamia, for example, temples to god and goddess couples were often built side by side, honoring the divine energies as intimate partners: Inanna and

Dumuzi, Ishtar and Tammuz. As Samuel Kramer, Helmar Ringgren, and other researchers of ancient religions have shown, the blessing derived from the "sacred marriage" spread out from the "bridal chamber" to the land, bringing fertility and well-being to people and to their crops and herds.

Liturgical poetry from ancient Sumer found on clay tablets honors the sacred union of the goddess Inanna with her consort Dumuzi, and mythology records the names of many other divine couples: Ishtar and Tammuz, Ba'al and Astarte, Isis and Osiris, Cybele and Attis. Though the stories of these deities differ in some respects, they have significant elements in common, such as the celebration of the nuptials of the pair; the sacrificial death of the bridegroom/king; and the joyful garden reunion of the separated couple at the site of his resurrection. In the elements of marriage, death, and resurrection, the myths of these pagan gods and goddesses manifest a remarkable resemblance to the story told of Jesus and Mary Magdalene in the Christian Gospels. Beginning with the anointing of Jesus by the woman with precious nard at the banquet at Bethany, and culminating with the reunion of Jesus and Mary on Easter morning recounted in John 20:14–17, the passion sequence follows the familiar pattern of the ancient cults. Regarded in this context, it seems apparent that the couple reunited in the garden bears the ancient archetypes of bride and bridegroom—the beloveds.

What happened to the ancient paradigm imaging the Divine as comprising the masculine and feminine, indeed as the union of sacred partners? Research in the fields of cultural anthropology and archaeology in recent decades by Marija Gimbutas and other scientists has uncovered unsuspected secrets of our remote ancestors buried under layers of drifting sand and rubble. Some of these discoveries have gone far to revise our view of history and the importance of the feminine principle devalued over the millennia since the time before history when the Divine was honored as feminine as well as masculine.

According to Marija Gimbutas and her followers, it was from their observations of the life-giving functions of the female that our Neolithic ancestors postulated the existence of a mother goddess whose domain was the bountiful planet Earth and whose abundance provided early humankind with the things needed for living. She was Mother of All. As Gimbutas has shown, very early in human history, as far back as 20,000 years ago, this goddess was represented in cave art and sculpture, usually with wide hips and ample breasts to celebrate her fertility. Primitive peoples who honored the goddess hunted and gathered food by daylight, then squatted at their fires in the evening, noting the ebb and flow of life, the cycles of the seasons, the freezing and thawing, the budding and harvesting, the birthing and dying. These prehistoric nomads gradually learned to till the fields and build shelters, settling in villages, fashioning artifacts of clay and straw, acknowledging the Great Mother as the source of all blessing. She was celebrated as the giver of some of civilization's greatest gifts: horticulture, crafts, arts, and even language itself.

MOTHER OF ALL

In *The Lost Language of Symbolism,*[1] Harold Bayley, a scholar of cultural anthropology and linguistics, notes that the sound represented by the letter *M* is the syllable *em* that represents the Mother Goddess as primeval water—the ocean presumed to be the source of all life on Earth. The word for "mother" in languages stemming from Indo-European begins with this sound, perhaps because it is so often the first sound that a human baby makes and is therefore equated with a cry for its mother. The word *mother* (*matr* in Sanskrit, *mater* in Latin) shares the same root with *matter* and *material*, and stands equally for our physical humanity, our flesh and bones formed in our mother's womb, and the essential elements and molecules of all material creation. Other words deriving from the same root include *matron, matri-*

archal, and even *matrimony,* all intimately involved with mother-hood, the "doorway" through which matter receives life and form.

Associations of the sound *em* with the "mother" are found in many religions. In the Greek texts of the Christian Gospels, the mother of Jesus is called Maria, while in Hebrew, she would be called Miriam; in Buddhism, the mother of Buddha is Maya; the mother of the Greek god Hermes is Maia; the Egyptian goddess of justice and principle of order is called Maat. According to Bayley, the sound *em* is widely associated with the primeval waters of the ocean and with the Great Mother. This sound is also fundamentally related to the cosmic "hum"—the sound of the constant interplay or dance of the cosmic energies represented by the Sanskrit *OM* (*aum*). And this sound seems also to be related to the archetype for mother, the *womb* itself. In the Greek alphabet, the letter Ω, omega, appears to mean "the great Om" and the Greek letter even assumes the physical silhouette of the creative cavity of womb—the archetypal "grail-chalice." While other letters can also be associated with a vessel, the omega seems to be the most suggestive of the physiology of the womb.

In the Book of Revelation, God says, "I am the Alpha and the Omega," the "first and last," the "beginning and the end" (Rev. 1:8). The alpha or "great A" of the masculine and the omega "Ω" of the archetypal feminine together represent the union of the opposites and the sum total of all creation contained in the essence of the ultimate and supreme Holy One—the wholeness of the divine monad. The other letters of the alphabet—representing the entire creation—are contained between these two, the first and last sounds of the Greek alphabet. Symbolically, the letters of the alphabet are sacred because they represent the entire generative "Word" of God calling forth the cosmos, their numerous combinations and variations seen as an infinite expression of the creative force.

Associations of the primeval mother with salt water precede by millennia our modern era's scientific confirmation that life on

Earth originated in the ocean, possibly as a result of volcanic action and intense heat underwater. In both Greek and Latin alphabets the letter that stands for the sound *em* takes the form of the waves of the sea, and the Hebrew letter *mem* means "water." In Latin *mare* means "ocean," and in Hebrew *mara* is "the bitter salt-sea."[2] All mammals are born from salt water, the amniotic fluid of their mother's womb. The word *mammal* (hence *mammary*) refers to those species of vertebrates that suckle their young and so echoes the feminine *mama*.

THE V AND THE Λ

Ancient shrines to the Great Mother goddess are found in numerous sites in Europe. Recent discoveries suggest that in certain Neolithic shrines dating from 7000 B.C. to 3500 B.C., the shape of the letter *V* is associated with the Mother Goddess.[3] A study of archaic symbolism suggests that perhaps the primeval *V* is the prehistoric symbol for the vessel or womb of all life—the archetypal chalice symbolic of the eternal Feminine and of our mother planet, for Earth is the sacred container and creative vessel of life as we know it.

In his work *Ancient Pagan and Modern Christian Symbolism*, first printed in 1868, Thomas Inman classified the prehistoric symbols for male and female found in ancient shrines all over the world. The rocks and "high places," and eventually the altars and pyres of sacrifice, are phallic shrines; while caves, grottoes, and crevices are associated with the orifices of the feminine. The great "A" or Δ, a three-dimensional tetrahedron or pyramid, represents the procreative power of the Great Father, the "ever-green One" often equated with the sun or fire god, whose cults, not surprisingly, frequently include pyramid building and a hierarchical priesthood derived from the absolute authority of the enthroned solar principle.

The symbolic counterpart of the male pyramid or triangle is

the ▽, the feminine or "water triangle," a vessel representing the Great Mother, Gaia herself. In mythologies of the ancient world, our planet is the receiver of the procreative action of the sun god. The Earth Goddess, impregnated by the rays of the sun, spreads a banquet for her children, bringing forth bountiful harvests of fruit and grain. Together the great △ and ▽, representing solar god and earth goddess, are united in a sacred harmony renewing the cycles of life on the planet. And in their intimate intertwining the symbols form a hexagram—✡—the archetypal image of the sacred marriage.

The regular hexagram or seal of Solomon, whose intrinsic meaning has long been obscured in Western consciousness, was honored in many of the ancient cultures of the world. It is an intimate interlacing of the archetypal symbols for male and female, the V (chalice) and the Λ (blade). It is also the symbol used in alchemy to represent the union of fire and water, whose glyphs are △ fire and water ▽. An early home of this symbol representing the cosmic dance of the opposite energies seems to have been India, where it symbolizes the sacred marriage of the Indian god Shiva and his goddess counterpart Shakti. It represents the eternal interplay of the positive and negative forces in all creation recognized as the cosmic dance.

Reference to the same symbol can be found in Western sources as well. In his book on sacred geometry, Danish mathematician Tons Brunés suggests that the phrase "the same and the different," discussed at length in Plato's *Timaeus*, characterized two identical triangles, the difference being that one is upright, the other inverted, forming a hexagram.[4] Triangles were considered the original building blocks of the universe in the philosophy of the ancients, so depiction of Plato's union of "the Same and the Other" as two triangles seems logical. It confirms the hexagram, ✡, as the symbol for "fusion"—Plato's term for the harmony or "marriage" of the opposites.[5] The male △ represents fire, possibly because its sharp edges were painful, and perhaps also because it was shaped like a flame tapering upward. Unconsciously it reflects the ancient awe caused by encounter with an active volcano spewing its terrifying and deadly fire. The opposite shape, the feminine ∇, symbolizes water in the esoteric tradition. Together, expressed as a regular hexagram, these two triangles represent the *yang* and *yin* that is based on the most ancient complementary relationship of all, the creative interplay of masculine and feminine energies.

FIRE AND THE MOUNTAIN

In *When God Was a Woman*, Merlin Stone postulates that the Indo-Aryan invaders from the east and north brought their male "fire" gods with them when they conquered the matrilineal peoples of the Near East. Perhaps they derived their god of power and might, fire and light, from an encounter with an angry fire mountain, an erupting volcano vomiting heat and molten lava from its mouth.[6] The volcano, according to this theory, would be the prototypical fire god who rules by power, violence, and intimidation. This hypothesis fits exactly the idea of the fire triangle as the archetypal symbol for the male power principle and the fact that sacrificial holocausts were so universally offered on altars, mounds, and pyres.

The same Δ is often found represented by a phallic pillar or carved stone sticking up out of the ground. These prehistoric mounds or altars, the "high places" of biblical anathema, and phallic *lingam* were honored as male shrines in India and the Middle East. Pyramids and pyres were characteristically built to a solar deity. Like Abraham in the Book of Genesis, builders of the pyres believed that the powerful fire god required propitiation in the form of burnt sacrifices. The word *pyramid*, from the Greek, has as its root *pyr*, which means fire. The identification of the sounds of the consonants *p* and *r* with the archaic worship of the male sun/fire god and the pyramid is made by Harold Bayley in his book *The Lost Language of Symbolism*: "The pyramid or cone was apparently at one time a universal symbol of the Primal Fire."[7] Both Plutarch and Plato equated the pyramid with fire. What may have originated in prehistoric times as the worship of an active volcanic "fire mountain" eventually became the cult of a wrathful male deity, even in terrain where no actual volcanic eruptions threatened.

The research of Marija Gimbutas and other anthropologists suggests that regions with bountiful harvests, abundant rainfall, and generally temperate conditions are apt to have evolved religions based on a loving and generous Earth goddess, while the tribes of arid steppes and deserts, where the realities of life are harsh and unaccommodating, are less likely to have formed a relationship with this bountiful goddess image and instead have often worshiped dominating and angry warrior gods. The classical roots of Western civilization are predominantly Greek, and Western mythologies and religions are fundamentally those of the Hellenized world of the Mediterranean basin where the intense sun was most often equated with the masculine/Logos principle and its solar attributes of power, reason, and light. This ascendant male principle gradually relegated the Great Mother goddess of Neolithic peoples to inferior status in the Greek pantheon, where Zeus was the all-powerful male ruler and Hera was his jilted and betrayed wife.

In the wake of the reorganization of civilizations along patriarchal lines that followed the Aryan invasions from the north, many empires since 3000 B.C. have been ruled by a dictator wielding absolute power, an oriental potentate acting as vicar or surrogate of an omnipotent sky-ruler of the universe. This father god of thunder, power, and might is envisioned heaving his lightning bolts from the sky or perhaps modeled, as previously suggested, on the angry fire god resident in a primeval volcano. The fire triangle has prevailed as the preeminent model for governmental and religious institutions all over the globe—the establishment—based on the absolute power of the leader at the top of the pyramid—Rome's Caesar, the pope, the commander-in-chief. The upward-pointing triangle is the model for the "establishment," founded on the root word *stable*, governed by strict rules and often by intimidation. And the V, the archetypal vessel representing the sacred feminine, has been systematically devalued during the same millennia—to the deep deprivation of all the children of Earth.

THE HIEROS GAMOS RESTORED

Realizing that the worship of an exclusively male image of God is both distorted and dangerous, we struggle to articulate attributes and images of God, trying to express the idea that god/goddess is not an "either/or" but a "both/and"—a supreme being whose essence manifests both masculine and feminine attributes. For too long we have depicted God as an old man with a beard, an exclusively male/father image similar to Michelangelo's portrayal of God on the ceiling of the Sistine Chapel or perhaps bearing a benevolent resemblance to Santa Claus.

Yet many passages from Hebrew Scripture refer to God with feminine attributes, like a mother who will never forget her child (Isa. 49:15). Medieval mystics including Hildegard von Bingen and Jacob Boehme expressed this same theme in some of their revelations. God's nature might be better understood to be an integrated wholeness, including both male and female attributes, both bride and bridegroom. Two sacred principles are at work: power and love. In democracy, founded on the principles of equality, justice, and freedom, the "establishment" is united with the "V"—the people—in a covenant modeled on the ✡ of the sacred marriage. This form of government ideally weds the various elements of society into a creative union under the rule of law.

Perhaps now, as we are opening to a new era of equality in many areas of life and society, it is time to reclaim the ancient paradigm for partnership and wholeness symbolized by the star of the hieros gamos. This star of partnership is present already in the Great Seal of the United States, placed by the founding fathers in the mandala of the thirteen stars that represent the first colonies.

The restoration of this ancient symbol of the hieros gamos as a model for peace and well-being could bring about a new Golden Age. As this profound image of integrated wholeness crystallizes, lodging in a single heart and spreading out into the land, it brings healed relationships and harmony. Jungian studies in psychology teach the integration and healing of the psyche when the inner energies of masculine and feminine are encouraged to develop and to coexist in partnership. That same principle, extended into the entire human community, could beome the model for wholeness for the promised "peaceful millennium." The image of God as partners creates streams of living water flowing out into the desert, healing the wasteland.

The ✡ paradigm for intimate union and partnership is the lost blueprint of the cosmic temple. Until it is restored in our consciousness, imprinting in us the mutual covenant of the archetypal bride and bridegroom, our planet will continue to be in danger of becoming a wasteland whose resources are exploited to exhaustion. Conscious now of the imminent threat we observe forests destroyed, waters polluted, fish poisoned, and resources squandered with blatant disregard. Gradually we are awakening to the plight of the "vessel" of our life. As we begin to cultivate the partnership paradigm in our own hearts, our homes, and our communities, we will begin to enjoy the "reign of God" promised in the Gospels, the peaceful millennium that is the prayer of every Christian heart throughout the ages: "Thy kingdom come!" It was a profound and fundamental teaching of Jesus that this kingdom was already in our midst awaiting only our awakening to the blessings of its presence.

Our study provides further insight concerning the eternal principle of harmony of the opposites, the sacred marriage that is of paramount importance in understanding certain hidden teachings of Jesus and his closest friends. Let us turn now to examine the powerful influence of the ancient cosmology on the Hellenized Roman Empire and the first-century authors of the Greek New Testament. We will first want to examine the ancient canon of sacred number and the measurements of the temple as they reflect cosmic reality. We will return later to the evidence supporting the union of the archetypal Christ-couple, Jesus and the Mary called the Magdalene.

2

THE CANON
OF NUMBER

Before we can attempt to understand the deeper meaning available to us in the gematria of the New Testament Greek, we must examine the concept of sacred geometry and the canon of symbolic number used by classical philosophers and mathematicians. These related subjects shed light on the development of religious consciousness in the first century of the current era, at the precise moment in time when Jesus of Nazareth was preaching in the streets of Judea.

Although much material has been published on this subject in recent years, many dedicated Scripture scholars are unaware of the secret meanings hidden in cherished New Testament phrases, secrets linked to the ancient canon of number and the esoteric practice of sacred geometry in the classical world. In a later chapter we shall focus on individual phrases of the New Testament that contain encoded hidden messages, but first we must understand the basis of this sacred geometry—literally, the "measurement of the earth"—in the wisdom of the ancients. Let us consider carefully their meticulous measurements of the cosmos and of its microcosm, the temple, which served for them as a reflection of ultimate reality.

The word *temple* has interesting etymological origins. Apparently the word stems from the Latin *temperare*, the source of the verb *temper*, which means to modify or balance as to proportion, as in the sense of tempering steel or tempering justice with mercy. The Latin *templum* was designed to reflect the power and attributes of the god or goddess whom it was erected to honor, and thus a temple designates the sacred space used for religious ritual while it also reflects the idea of balancing and controlling certain energies by means of the careful attention to measurements and ratios in the architectural design. It is these very concerns that are at the heart of the sacred geometry of the ancient mathematicians. The sublime temples whose columns ascend heavenward into the sunny skies of Mediterranean lands make visible this desire to harmonize and "temper" the energies of the gods and channel them into human communities. Another word related to this same stem is *template*—a model, guide, or pattern used in creating something according to a specific design. A temple is conceived precisely as such a guide or pattern, created to hold the cosmic principles of the universe in its blueprint.

SYNCRETISM IN THE ROMAN EMPIRE

Archaeologists have noted the similarities of classic temples in many lands of the Mediterranean basin. This is not surprising, since the Near East from Egypt to India was conquered by the Macedonian ruler Alexander the Great in the fourth century B.C. The similarity of the region's temples built during and after Alexander's reign attests to the syncretism or cultural borrowing and cross-fertilization that occurred during the several centuries of the Greek Empire, a period spanning nearly three hundred years until 31 B.C., the date most commonly given for the beginning of Roman hegemony over the region whose shores are washed by the Mediterranean Sea.

The assimilation of Greek culture during these centuries of

Greek influence, including the borrowing and sharing of religious beliefs and cult practices, was so widespread that foreign gods and goddesses adopted by disparate cities of the empire shared attributes with former deities indigenous to each locality. Sacred shrines and temples were renamed and consecrated to the new deities, and the mythologies of both old and new became interwoven, a practice repeated in Christianity's later adoption of pagan holy sites for its own shrines and cathedrals. Names and attributes of the pagan deities, their feast days and festivals, and their rites, taboos, and blessings were borrowed, shared, and amalgamated across the entire known world.

We are aware that the Greek father god Zeus was called Jupiter in Rome and that the moon goddess Diana, the huntress, was the Roman equivalent of the Greek goddess and huntress Artemis, two of the many cases of shared identity among the ancients' deities. The Greek love goddess Aphrodite was Venus in Rome, while Hermes, the messenger god of the Greeks, was identified with Mercury, and the Greek war god Ares with the Roman Mars. This practice of superimposing the cultural values and deities of the conqueror upon those of the conquered, far older than history, is the natural result of assimilation through the formation of "frontier" settlements and the intermarriage of the conquerors with the subjugated peoples.

The Acropolis that crowns the hill above Athens and other temple ruins of the Mediterranean region display graceful marble pillars silhouetted against an azure sky. But these majestic temple structures were not designed just to look beautiful or to inspire awe. Each temple was built as a dwelling place for the power and attributes of the god or goddess whom the region's residents wished to invoke as a patron or benefactress. And attracting the power of the god or goddess to the temple was not a hit-or-miss proposition. The theology of the pagans was part of an intricate system that included a canon of sacred number. By 500 B.C., the spelling of the name of each deity in the Greek pantheon had been standardized to include its mathematical value or "sacred number." These numbers were then reflected in the measurements of the temple built to attract the favor of a particular divinity. This principle as it applies to the Parthenon in Athens has been carefully computed and tabulated by David Fideler in his book *Jesus Christ, Sun of God.* In addition to their impressive pillars and beautiful marble statuary, the actual physical measurements of the ancient temples and standing stones (dolmen) merit careful scrutiny, for they cast light on the religious beliefs and cosmology of the people who designed them, just as the cathedrals of medieval Europe reflect the mind-set and faith of their architects, construction engineers, and masons. As we shall see, the exact measurements and sacred numbers derived by the mathematicians of the ancient world may be of tremendous importance in understanding early New Testament documents.

SACRED NUMBERS IN THE ANCIENT WORLD

Early in my own spiritual journey I stumbled upon the principles of sacred geometry but could not hope to fully fathom the symbolic meaning of measurements of temples long in ruins. The task was monumental! Fascinated by the subject, I began the search by noticing scriptural references to significant numbers. It was clear that numbers were not chosen at random. In the Hebrew Bible the most prominent number that first demanded my attention appears, predictably, in Genesis—the number seven, so prevalent in ethical and religious terminology in the ancient Near East: " . . . and on the seventh day, God rested" (Gen. 2:2).

Among the Greeks, seven is called the "virgin" number because it is neither a multiple nor a factor of any of the other of the first ten numbers. The number ten was represented by Greek geometers in the figure of the *tetractys*—a triangular figure of four units on each side—from which all other numbers and all creation were said to have been generated. Ten, the sum of the numbers from one to four, is also a "triangular" number, which

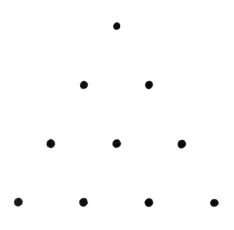

Figure 2.1. *The* tetractys *of the Pythagoreans.*

can be illustrated by arranging ten dots as an equilateral triangle in four rows: the top is a single dot followed by rows containing two, three, and then four dots. According to Greek cosmology, an equilateral triangle is the basic building block of the universe.

THE FIRST ELEMENTS OF GEOMETRY

Tons Brunés has offered an interesting explanation that relates to the heavenly properties of seven and to its associations with the Goddess and the moon, showing how the menstrual feminine (lunar) cycle of twenty-eight days related to the basic human digits.[1] According to his analysis, the first numbers used by human beings were the numbers one to twenty, corresponding to fingers and toes. Units of measurement were in all likelihood as simple as a man's foot, his stride, and his thumb joint. A fathom, the length between his fingertips with his arms outstretched, was six feet. Because the size of a typical man's foot does not vary widely from one culture to another, the basic measurements of the ancient civilizations Egypt, Greece, and Rome were very similar. For example, a Greek foot measures 1.008 of an English foot. The basic assumptions concerning the origins of measurement hypothesized by Tons Brunés are confirmed by archaeological evidence.

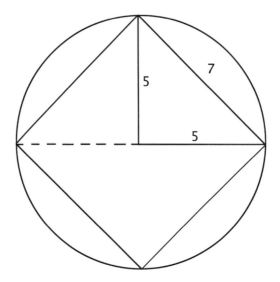

Figure 2.2. The "sun circle" of primitive peoples
illustrates the divisions of the lunar month. A circle with
the diameter of 10 units divided into four equal segments
has chords of approximately 7 units.

Brunés postulates that the first symbol used by our ancestors
was most probably the circle, the "sun" symbol ubiquitous across
the globe.[2] He suggests that the radius of the circle measured 5,
the number of digits on a human hand. As shown in figure 2.2,
when a circle having a diameter of 10 units is divided into quarters by a cross through the center, each arm of the cross
measures 5 units, and the chord drawn between two of the arms
(the hypotenuse of each of the four right triangles formed)
measures only slightly more than 7 units (approximating the
square root of 50).

This original division of the circle into quarters reflected the
actual phases of the moon in its seven day intervals, and the
lunar month of twenty-eight days that governs the menstrual
flow of women can similarly be divided into four equal segments
of seven days each. Thus, the association of the number seven
with the sacred feminine and the lunar aspects of "virgin" and the

moon goddess is reinforced. Brunés suggests that this elementary mathematical discovery was probably the foundation of all later inventions and may lie at the root of the cyclical symbolism of the number seven among ancient peoples who adopted a week of seven days reflected in the Book of Genesis: "So God blessed the seventh day and made it holy" (Gen. 2:3).

To the naked eye of our remote ancestors, only seven luminous bodies were visible in the heavens—the sun and moon and five planets. Pythagoras named seven tones on the musical scale, and later seven liberal arts were identified. Seven wonders of the world were praised, seven chakras proclaimed, and seven demons typically expelled.

In Hebrew law and scriptures, seven was the sacred number of completeness of a time cycle. The people of the covenant worshiped Yahweh, their unseen deity, on the Sabbath, the seventh day, which was marked as a day of rest. By analogy, it took Solomon seven years to complete the Temple in Jerusalem. Many Jewish festivals were celebrated for a period of seven days, and seven weeks occurred between the feast of the unleavened bread (Passover) and the feast of the leavened bread (Pentecost). This latter feast was begun on the fiftieth day, the "jubilee day" after the elapse of "a week of weeks" (7×7 days = 49 days plus one added day—the fiftieth day celebrated as the "jubilee").

In the Book of Leviticus we find a command of Yahweh to Moses concerning the land: "When you enter the land that I am giving to you, let the land, too, keep a Sabbath for the Lord. For six years you may sow your field and for six years prune your vineyard . . . but during the seventh year the land shall have a complete rest" (Lev. 2–4). In Israel a field was cultivated for six years and allowed by law to lie fallow during the seventh—which was called the "sabbatical year." A cycle of seven "sabbatical" years—a total cycle of forty-nine years—was followed in Israel by a fiftieth year when no work was done, no fields planted. It was to be a "jubilee" year of thanksgiving and merrymaking to honor the gracious bounty of God. In this fiftieth year, all slaves were to be set free, all debts forgiven, all grudges forgotten, and the slate rubbed clean so that in the fifty-first year a whole new cycle could commence: "This fiftieth year you shall make sacred by proclaiming liberty in the land of all its inhabitants . . . you shall not sow nor shall you reap the aftergrowth" (Lev. 25:10–11).

Some of these uses of the number seven are familiar—the feasts of Easter and Pentecost in the Christian calendar are derived from the great harvest feasts of the leavened and unleavened bread from the Jewish calendar, hence the fifty days separating the two holy days. In medieval times, an apprentice served his artisan master for seven years and then continued to serve as a journeyman for another seven before himself becoming a master. Other familiar uses of seven-year periods are found in the term of servitude of indentured servants and the "sabbatical" leave of professors, a period allowing them to "lie fallow." Even today children "come of age" at twenty-one after three complete cycles of seven years.

Seven saw a time cycle completed, but it was also the number of eternity and of spiritual completeness or perfection. In Greek tradition it was the virgin number associated with Pallas Athene and Holy Wisdom, while in Christian tradition it is the number often associated with the Holy Spirit, whose gifts are sevenfold. There are seven spiritual works of mercy and seven cardinal sins. Jesus said we should forgive not seven times, but seventy times seven!

The perfection inherent in the number seven is illustrated in figure 2.3, an ancient diagram known as "the Seed of Life," which shows a sixfold pattern containing six circles (representing all of physical creation—the entire cosmos!) with a seventh circle having the same radius drawn connecting the centers of the other six, uniting them into a spiritual wholeness. Such are the subtleties of sacred geometry, which uses shape and symmetry to express deeper realities.

Figure 2.3. *The seven circles of the "Seed of Life" mandala.*

The sixfold pattern of the "Seed of Life" symbol with its six connected *vesica piscis* petals echoes the hexagram representing the
sacred union of the masculine and feminine—the source of life
on Earth, while the seventh circle represents the spiritual dimension of reality.

FORTY DAYS AND FORTY NIGHTS

In addition to seven, the numbers four and forty occur often in
the Judiac-Christian Scriptures. Four was considered feminine
and was associated with matter and the physical world, in contrast to the irrational and volatile properties of three, the first
masculine number. The basic elements were four: fire, water, air,
and earth. The physical planet was said to have four corners from
which the four winds blew, the four cardinal points of the com-
pass. Among the Greeks, four represented the rational properties
of a square, and the planet Earth was often envisioned as flat and
square. Four seasons were noted, and four distinct ages of the
world. There were four temperaments identified in members of
the human family, and four humors.

Associated with four, the number forty occurs naturally in the life cycles of human beings; for instance, the gestation of a human child in the womb is forty weeks—the "incubation period"—and the common life expectancy of a human being was traditionally perceived to be forty years. During the Flood, Noah and his family lived with their menagerie in the ark for forty days and forty nights. Jesus spent forty days being tested in the desert, a reminder of the trials of the Hebrew people who wandered for forty years, one entire generation, in the desert after their dramatic escape from Pharaoh over the dry path through the Red Sea. The forty-day Lenten fast of Christians between Ash Wednesday and Easter is an echo of the forty-day period of Jesus' temptation in the desert (Matt. 4:1–2). The "mother" letter *M* discussed earlier has a numerical value of forty in both the Hebrew and Greek alphabet, and, in a further level of significance, 444 in the ancient canon was the numerical equivalent of the Greek phrase "flesh and blood" (σαρξ και αιμα) found in 1 Corinthians 15:50.[3]

Other significant numbers occur in the Bible and will be discussed in the chapters that follow. I have mentioned seven, four, and forty by way of illustrating something of the vastly important symbolic content of numbers in the Judiac-Christian tradition and among ancient peoples. Some of the symbolic meanings associated with the ten numbers of the *tetractys* were these:

> One, or the *monad*: wholeness and unity; solar principle; the Holy One
>
> Two, or the *dyad*: duality; division of the One into equal parts
>
> Three, or the *triad*: active, generative principle in nature; first "masculine" number
>
> Four, or the *tetrad*: symmetry, order, civilization, and matter; the first feminine number

Five, or the *pentad*: health and humanity, five senses, five extremities of the human body

Six, or the *hexad*: related to circle, solar time, creation, and the cosmos

Seven, or the *heptad*: "virgin" number; eternal things and time cycles (Athene)

Eight, or the *ogdoad*: first solid or cubic number, a cube with eight vertices; regeneration (gematria of Jesus/Ihsous = 888)

Nine, or the *ennead*: completion, end of a series; "truth" and "judgment"

Ten, or the *decad*: begins a new cycle, represents the created cosmos, the reflection of the monad on a lower plane.

TEMPLES OF OUR ANCESTORS

Modern scholars Louis Charpentier, Fred Gettings, and others have studied the measurements of the Gothic cathedrals of medieval Europe for examples of the principles of sacred geometry evident in their stones, and have compiled evidence that these cathedrals were laid out and constructed according to principles that governed the construction of the ancient temples of the Mediterranean, and many medieval churches were built according to similar principles of sacred geometry. Pyramids and standing stones provide ample evidence that the practice of symbolic architecture is far older than the Greek temples of classical antiquity. The solar orientation of the standing stones of Stonehenge and the burial mound at Newgrange in Ireland has been passionately researched and documented. One suggested theory is that circles of standing stones and other ancient monuments may have been designed as calendars, accurately marking the solstices and equinoxes for the prehistoric peoples who built them, to help them accurately track the seasons. The standing stones testify to the marvelously precise knowledge of mathematics and astronomy employed by their builders and to a concern with the recurring cycles of the sun, moon, and seasons. Their careful measurements often provide evidence for the basic numbers of the canon revered in early civilizations and have proved valuable in determining the significance of symbolic numbers. In *The Dimensions of Paradise,* John Michell provides profound evidence that the dimensions of the New Jerusalem from the Book of Revelation are based on the same pattern and measurements as the basic design of Stonehenge, built nearly two thousand years before. The basic circumference of Stonehenge—3168—is also the numerical value of the most sacred name in Christianity—"Lord Jesus Christ."

Often the foundations of the earliest temples were oriented so that the rays of the rising sun, usually on the day of the summer or winter solstice, or occasionally on a festival day of the deity (or later, a patron saint), would penetrate into the innermost sanctuary of the temple, the "womb," tabernacle, or Holy of Holies. This generative action of the sun consummated the symbolic marriage of heaven and earth, or of a god and the community, bringing the two opposites together in a fruitful union that then emanated from the "bridal chamber" at the center of the temple out into the surrounding lands, blessing the entire community. At the Neolithic mound excavated at Newgrange, built probably 5,200 years ago, a shaft of light from the rising sun on the day of the winter solstice penetrates the long passageway leading to the inner sanctum and illuminates a series of sun glyphs on the back wall of the chamber, which one can speculate was perhaps intended to be the path guiding the spirit of the dead to new life in the eternal celestial sphere. According to Jewish Kabbalists, the Holy of Holies in the Temple of Jerusalem was perceived as a bridal chamber where the Yahweh was united with his Shekhinah, often characterized as the "feminine manifestation" or "immanence" of God.

To align a sacred structure in such a way that the sun pene-
trated into its innermost chamber or tabernacle on a significant
feast day or as a way to mark the exact date of the summer or
winter solstice was in itself a monumental feat of astronomy,
mathematics, and engineering. The practice was not confined to
pagan temples, sacred mounds, and grottoes of the ancient
world, but was reintroduced by medieval architects and masons
who carried on the ancient practice used by the architects of the
ancient Near East and perpetuated its use in Western Europe.
Numerous cathedrals and chapels built in the Middle Ages seem
to have been oriented toward the sun or some special arrange-
ment of the planets at their date of origin,[4] and symbolic
numbers from the Scriptures and the ancient canon are often
reflected in their measurements, as at Chartres, where the
length of the famous labyrinth path formed in the stones of the
nave is 666 feet. This number is of particular interest because it
occurs in the Book of Revelation where it bears an ugly stigma as
the "number of the beast." We will discuss in a later chapter the
solar properties of the number 666, which seem, at Chartres, to
be invoked in an attempt to balance the strongly feminine associations of the labyrinth's path as the pattern for the inward
journey.

Louis Charpentier has established that the cathedral at
Chartres was built on a seven-sided pattern, reflecting the Holy
Sophia, the virgin/wisdom archetype embodied in the sacred feminine.[5] In his book on Chartres, Charpentier reflects on the
standard provided by the "Druid's cord," one of the most basic tools
of ancient geometers. This ingenious measuring line was knotted
at twelve equal intervals so that it had thirteen equal segments. By
laying the cord out in a triangle with three segments on one side,
four on the second, and five on the third, a Pythagorean or right triangle could be constructed. An isosceles triangle could also be
constructed with the cord, each side having four segments with
five segments in the base. The angles at the base of this isosceles

triangle provided the 51.2° angle that very nearly demarcates the seventh part of a circle (which angle is 51.43°), and it was used to form heptagonal figures in ancient times.

THE ARK, THE HEXAGRAM, AND THE TEMPLE

The secrets of number and geometry were passed down to temple initiates whose sacred duty it was to preserve the knowledge imparted in secrecy, for knowledge was power! The portable tabernacle known as the Ark of the Covenant, designed to represent the presence of Yahweh accompanying the Israelites during their forty years of wandering in the desert, has been shown to contain significant mathematical secrets that Moses may have studied as a nobleman and temple initiate in Egypt.[6] According to Tons Brunés, Moses was apparently initiated into the lore and secrets of Egypt, and it is possible that the exact measurements of the tabernacle reported in the Book of Exodus to have been revealed to the charismatic leader of the Israelites on Mount Sinai actually encoded treasured secrets of geometry, the composite research of centuries of initiates in the temples of Egypt. Moses is believed to have learned this closely guarded lore during his sojourn as the adopted son of Pharaoh's daughter and to have coded it into specific measurements of the Ark of the Covenant, the curtains of the tabernacle, the altar, and the table used for the ritual showbreads described in the Book of Exodus.

Jewish rabbinical tradition teaches that the Ark of the Covenant kept in the Holy of Holies of Solomon's Temple on Mount Zion in Jerusalem contained, in addition to the tablets on which the Ten Commandments were inscribed, a "man and a woman locked in intimacy in the form of a hexagram"—the intimate union of the opposites.[7] The inherent meaning of the hexagram, the mutuality or harmony of the opposites, is summed up in the Hebrew greeting *shalom*, meaning "peace and well-being." The sacred ✿ sheltered in the Ark of the Covenant survived in rabbinical tradition as the preeminent symbol for sacred marriage, a promise of the covenant of Yahweh and his people, and a mandala for "a land flowing with milk and honey," an esoteric image mentioned in the Book of Exodus in the description of the Promised Land to be granted to the people of Israel as their new homeland. The land so abundantly blessed celebrated the fullness of God and the union and wholeness of creation. In ancient Sumerian poetry celebrating the hieros gamos, milk and honey are symbolic of the erotic secretions of male and female partners during coitus. So the epithet "milk and honey" conveys the joyful spirit of conjugal harmony, fruitfulness, and well-being in the language of symbol. This is the land where people live "happily ever after" because the harmonious balance of the opposites is celebrated at the core of the community.

The intimate union of the masculine and feminine energies, the cosmic dance of the polarities, was the source of all harmony in the universe. And bees, whose matriarchal society produces the delicious and valuable gift of honey, were recognized totems for the goddesses in the ancient world. Perhaps their hum was perceived as a distant echo of the cosmic hum—the great *OM*. In a community of honeybees the *melissae,* or females, surround and protect the queen. This feminine association of bees was known and honored in ancient times: priestesses of the goddess Artemis were called *melissae,* and Demeter was called "the pure Mother Bee." In Hebrew, the name of Deborah, one of the great Old Testament heroines, means "queen bee." Honey was held sacred for its heavenly sweetness as well as its miraculous power as a preservative. The only other known preservative was salt.

A land of milk and honey is clearly a country filled with nature's bounty. It is a land where children are nurtured, widows consoled, foreigners made welcome, and arts and letters, music, and dance encouraged. In this land, childhood is joyful, work productive, and people live in harmony. The land of milk and honey is a society that knows the secret of the universe—

the honeycomb of sweetness found at the center of the ✡ of sacred union. I suspect that our English word "honeymoon" is far more than just a nice vacation celebrated by newlyweds. Very likely it is a memory fossil of the consummation of the nuptials found in the hexagonal center of this model for partnership and mutuality.

The association of bees with the Greek goddesses Aphrodite, Artemis, and Demeter in the temples of antiquity is suitably reinforced by the insects' ability to form perfect hexagons in the combs where their honey is stored. This sacred shape has long been considered a stable and subtle form in the created universe. Crystals of water when frozen form six-pointed stars, and six also was sacred to the goddesses Isis and Aphrodite. The ancient philosophers understood that the basic building blocks of the universe were triangular, not dualistic (linear), an understanding reflected in their view of the cosmos as multifaceted and their mythologies that illustrated many coexisting aspects of the Divine.

Honey, the distillation of nectar from many blossoms, was itself symbolic of wisdom, a synthesis that is not the result of mere intellectual activity, but rather something more than reason, more than "I.Q." Wisdom combines "head" knowledge with "heart" and integrates facts into a value system. It is the synthesis of masculine and feminine ways of knowing—reason or "left-brained" and intuition or "right-brained"—rendering the hexagram a fitting symbol for wisdom. The figure that encompasses a hexagram is the hexagon, the fundamental unit formed by bees in constructing their lattice—the "honey in the honeycomb." The Hebrew songwriter is filled with the praise of wisdom: "If you eat honey, my son, because it is good . . . if virgin honey is sweet to your taste, such you must know is wisdom to your soul" (Prov. 24:13–14); "The statutes of the Lord are true, all of them just; more desirable than gold . . . sweeter also than honey or drippings from the comb" (Ps. 19:10–11). Wisdom herself calls: "Come to me, all you that yearn for me, and be filled with my fruits; you will remember me as sweeter than honey, better than the honeycomb" (Sir. 24:19).

According to the Hebrew Bible, 480 years after the descendants of Jacob settled the area of what is now Israel, their wise king Solomon, favored son of King David and Bathsheba, commenced to honor God by building a temple in Jerusalem. Yahweh had told King David that a temple could not contain God because the entire cosmos was his, but in the fourth year of Solomon's reign in Israel, a temple was begun on Mount Zion under the supervision of Hiram, a man from Tyre who was an artificer in metals. Explicit descriptions of the Temple and its exact measurements, furnishings, and decorations are found in the Hebrew Scriptures in 1 Kings, including the pillars in the front, to be named Boaz and Jachin, meaning "established in strength" (1 Kings 7:21). The walls of the Temple were paneled with gold and its sanctuary overlaid with the same precious ore, as were the two carved cherubim that guarded the Ark of the Covenant and the altar within the Holy of Holies.

The Hebrew Bible also contains several references to the measurements of the Temple of Solomon in the prophetic books of Ezekiel (written in the sixth century) and Zechariah (c. 520), and the New Testament makes similar references in Revelation 21. In Ezekiel 39–41 "a man who shone like bronze" measures the walls, gateways, entrances, rooms, and passageways of the temple on Mount Zion in minute detail, and the measurements are recorded in the text. By contrast, the reference in Zechariah (2: 5–6) is short. It merely says that the prophet saw in a vision a man holding in his hand a measuring line (was this a knotted string similar to the Druid's cord? We are not told). The man in the vision said that he was going to measure Jerusalem to see how long and how wide it is. In the Greek New Testament the visionary author of Revelation is told to measure the Temple and the altar and to count those who worship there (Rev. 11:1); and in the same book, an angel with a measuring line measures the Holy City Jerusalem, its gates, and its wall (Rev. 21:15–17).

John Michell and others have shown that this attention to the measurements of God's dwelling place was not accidental but designed to convey special meaning to those initiated into the secret canon of the symbolic significance of number, also a fundamental tenet of the Greek contemporaries of the Hebrew prophets—the followers of Pythagoras (580–500 B.C.). Apparently the sages of both peoples derived their wisdom from the same ancient sources.

A revival of interest in these ancient principles has resulted in numerous works on the subjects of sacred geometry and numerology, spearheaded perhaps by the publication of John Michell's *The City of Revelation* in 1971. The further work of John Michell, Nigel Pennick, Tons Brunés, Robert Lawlor, Keith Critchlow, and others provides verification and documentation of the practice of the ancient mathematicians, philosophers, and Kabbalists and their systems of sacred number. The influence of the authentic sacred canon can also be found encoded in the Greek texts of the New Testament. Understanding these symbolic numbers is the secret key to the hidden reign of God that Jesus promised was already "in our midst." Or did he say that the kingdom was "within" us?

3

SACRED NUMBERS AND
THE NEW TESTAMENT

There is a tradition stemming from early writings of the patriarchs of the Christian church, still acknowledged by numerous Scripture scholars, that the Greek text of the final New Testament book, the Apocalypse of John, was "coded" in a way that, if correctly understood, would reveal important secret knowledge. For centuries no one seems to have known how to decipher the alleged secrets. Understanding the practice of gematria, however, enables us to break the codes of the Book of Revelation and the other New Testament texts, and sheds new light on the message of the Gospels and their intimate relationship to classical Greek philosophy and mathematics.

The libraries of the ancient world, most of them private collections that once held the key to the hidden tradition, were systematically destroyed during endless power struggles in the region. The persecutions of Christians, Gnostics, and pagans routinely included the burning of their libraries, since knowledge is universally synonymous with power. Some ancient texts were saved for posterity, however. The Dead Sea Scrolls of the Qumran community were hidden in earthen jars during the second-century

Jewish rebellion against the Romans, and a group of Gnostic texts was hidden near Nag Hammadi, Egypt, in about A.D. 400 to avoid certain destruction at the hands of pious, orthodox Christians. The armies of Islam sweeping across North Africa in the seventh century continued the cultural destruction by burning surviving libraries of classical antiquity. One of the Muslim generals is said to have ordered the burning of the famous public library in Alexandria, which had been destroyed several centuries previously, in 389. He is said to have justified his action by stating that if the books in the library did not agree with the Koran, they were blasphemous, and if they did, they were superfluous!

Later Arab intellectuals compiled and translated surviving works of classical philosophy and science in their own libraries, but these works were not widely available to Europeans in the Dark Ages. Scholars from the West encountered Arabic works in Spain's intellectual centers and during the Crusades, but not until the mid-fifteenth century, when Cosimo de' Medici of Florence collected and assembled a body of classical Greek, Latin, and Arabic texts and had them studied and translated, did the Christian world again have access to the wisdom of the ages. This blossoming of science and learning in the Renaissance was discouraged and sometimes threatened by the Holy Office of the Inquisition, as demonstrated by the trial of Galileo, a famous example of this repression of scientific exploration and research. Certain works were banned and burned by the Church, but many survived due to the courage and perseverance of scholars who copied and hid them.

The Greeks of the classical period were ardent advocates of harmony and equilibrium. The ruins of their architecture and art still reflect these fundamental values of their civilization, although the symbolic meanings of the measurements themselves are believed to have been lost. But in this age of computer technology, research dealing with numbers and numerology can be easily collated and accessed, facilitating the work of scholars who have sought to reconstruct the canon of sacred numbers. In a study of ancient measurement entitled *The Dimensions of Paradise*, John Michell published some of the sacred numbers of the ancient pagan cosmology, demonstrating that these numbers are reflected in the measurements of the New Jerusalem envisioned in the Book of Revelation.[1] Based on the works of Plato and other classical sources, Michell derives his numbers from geometry—the actual measurements of the radii, diameters, and circumferences of the sun, the moon, and the earth—and he demonstrates how the geometers of classical antiquity came into possession of these dimensions and numbers. Michell's books provide a virtual treasure trove of rediscovered esoteric wisdom.

Having established the paramount numbers sacred to the ancient cosmology, Michell correlates them with the ancient practice of gematria, the system of calculating the numerical value of words and phrases so that a particular epithet or phrase adds up to the numerical value of an established sacred cosmic principle.

GEMATRIA

The word gematria (derived from the Greek root for *geometry*—the measuring of the earth) does not appear in most modern dictionaries, a fact that points to the obscurity of the practice and the invisibility of its historical importance. Its first recorded use appears to have been in Babylon in the eighth century when Sargon II built the wall of Khorsabad 16,283 cubits long to correspond to the numerical value of his own name. The practice of gematria was common throughout the classical world, especially in the literature of the Persian Magi and by interpreters of dreams in the Hellenistic world. It was probably introduced into Hebrew writings during the period of the Second Temple (sixth to first centuries).

Gematria is a long-honored and well-honed literary device employed to enhance the subtle meaning of certain verses and phrases and possibly used as a mnemonic device as well. It required a deliberate manipulation of letters and words, similar to the rhyme scheme of a poem but more sophisticated. Instead of setting their verses to music, the authors of the sacred texts set them to number. Only an initiated elite could have fully understood and savored the meaning of many New Testament phrases enriched by gematria—those same individuals whom the Gospels mention as having "eyes to see and ears to hear." Certain of these familiar phrases—"a grain of mustard seed," "a pearl of great price," "fountain of wisdom"—illuminate secret teachings hidden for millennia in the numerically coded words of Jesus found in the Gospels and in other sacred texts of the New Testament.

Actually, the system of gematria was very simple. The twenty-seven letters of the Greek alphabet were arranged in three rows of nine letters. Three letters, *digamma, koppa,* and *sampi,* one letter from each of the rows, later fell out of use in the alphabet but were retained as number values. Each of the remaining twenty-four letters had a numerical value assigned to it, and the sum of a word or phrase could be easily calculated by adding together the values of its individual letters. Since an exact "correct" sum was often difficult to achieve in the spelling of a word or phrase, the calculated value in the classical system was allowed a leeway of +1 or –1, which difference was called the *colel.* Thus some gematria values are not precisely equal to the sacred cosmic number they were intended to symbolize, but may miss the exact total by the value of ±1 without altering their symbolic significance.

TABLE OF GREEK ALPHABET WITH NUMERICAL VALUES*

A,α	B,β	Γ,γ	Δ,δ	E,ε	Z,ζ	H,η	Θ,θ
1	2	3	4	5	7	8	9
I,ι	K,κ	Λ,λ	M,μ	N,ν	Ξ,ξ	O,o	Π,π
10	20	30	40	50	60	70	80
P,ρ	Σ,σ,ς	T,τ	Y,υ	Φ,φ	X,χ	Ψ,ψ	Ω,ω
100	200	300	400	500	600	700	800

*Three letters were obsolete by the time the New Testament was written: *digamma*, 6; *koppa*, 90; and *sampri*, 900. Although they do not occur in words and thus in gematria, they were retained for use as numbers.

Certain numbers were held sacred because they reflected the actual measurement of a significant celestial body. For example, 1080 approximated the radius of the moon in miles and was the long-established "lunar" number of the sacred feminine, according to the research of John Michell, while 7920 miles was the calculated diameter of the earth. If a square is drawn around a circle with a diameter of 7920 miles (to represent the earth), the square has a perimeter of 31,680, reflecting the sum of the Greek title "Lord Jesus Christ"—3168—which is also the number associated with the world-circumference in Pliny's *Natural History* —3,168,000 miles.[2] In the system of gematria, zeroes representing multiples of 10 do not alter the symbolic value of the measurement, so the World Soul and the perimeter of the square around the circumference of the earth have identical symbolic significance.

When a literary phrase or epithet added up to the number of the cosmic principle it reflected, it naturally emphasized the original meaning of a phrase, but on a higher plane. The practice enhanced verbal expression by giving it a mathematical and cosmological dimension reflecting its symbolic and literary value. In Hebrew, the system is based on twenty-two letters and is still practiced today among learned rabbis, who delight in weaving their sacred numbers into phrases of their teachings. Perhaps we should not be so surprised to learn that the Jewish rabbi Jesus practiced the same art, since gematria was far more commonly employed in his lifetime than in ours.

What can this ancient system of gematria do for us? How does it illuminate the meaning of the teachings found in the Greek New Testament writings of the first century? Can an esoteric meaning in Christ's teaching have been hidden all these years in the numerical values of the phrases he used? Is it possible that because we did not understand the gematria values attached to certain New Testament phrases, the fullness of their meaning has been obscured and even distorted? With the help of modern electronic computation, we can now access and correlate all the numerically coded phrases in the New Testament, and this, in fact, is being done!

ENHANCED TEACHINGS

Clearly if many ancient poets, teachers, and philosophers used the system of gematria, it was no idle practice; they must have thought it was an important method of enhancing the meaning of their text. And indeed, the deciphering of the coded numbers greatly enriches the message in the Greek words of the New Testament.

To illustrate this, let us examine a single word whose sacred number by gematria both reflects and deepens its meaning. For this example, we choose the word for "dove"—*peristera* in Greek. The Greek letters περιστερα add up to 801. The sum of the digits of this number added together is 9, the product of 3 × 3 or a "trinity of threes." All numbers were held sacred by the ancients, but three was one considered most holy. Triangles, as we have already noted, were believed by the Pythagoreans to be the fundamental building blocks of the universe.

But there is a mystical significance inherent in the number three as well: three times any number enhances the meaning of that number. Therefore, 3 × 3 would be the "epitome of three," ultimate holiness and truth! The lore of the Goddess often refers to her as the "triple goddess" (modeled on the threefold Hecate)—the "maiden, mother, and crone" aspects of the feminine, while Christianity teaches the worship of the Trinity or three-in-one God, so this sacredness of the number three should seem familiar. We are also attuned to the idea that "three times is the charm"; many feats in folklore and fairy tale are successful only on the third try, as in "Jack and the Beanstalk," in which the hero visits the ogre three times before destroying him, and often in such stories it is the third son who is the hero, like the simpleton in "Puss in Boots." Apparently the mystic connotations of "threeness" are universally sensed rather than rationally understood. While two surprising correspondences might be accidental, three are eerily coincidental or synchronistic. The spiritual connotations of the number three are extended to include nine—its square—and to the numbers like 1080 and 801 ("dove") that can be reduced to nine by adding their digits. It is noteworthy that many of the sacred numbers of the canon, derived from the actual measurements of the earth and then rounded to appropriate whole number values, resolve to nine when the sum of their digits is calculated: 7920, 3168, 1440, 1746, 1224—significant numbers that will be discussed in later chapters.

The number nine—"thrice holy"—represents "fulfillment," "completion," and "truth" in the system of gematria, and its related numbers carry similar but more powerful meanings. For example, written prayers of the early Christians often end with "99," the gematria for "Amen" ($A\mu\eta\nu$ in Greek)—"so be it." And 999 is considered the epitome of "nineness," or ultimate fulfillment: Judgment Day and the fulfillment of prophecy. From these preliminary examples we begin to appreciate how the symbolic meanings of these numbers may play on one another.

Returning to our first example, in classical times, the dove ($\pi\epsilon\rho\iota\sigma\tau\epsilon\rho\alpha$) with its gematria of 801 was the totem bird associated with the love goddess Venus/Aphrodite and also with Sophia, the goddess of wisdom. The presence of the doves in the pillared courtyards of the temples of these goddesses was renowned. This association is echoed in the Hebrew tradition in the Song of Songs, the liturgical poem of the sacred marriage, where the bridegroom addresses his beloved as "my dove."

The fundamental number associated with the moon goddess and with the feminine principle in general in the ancient canon was 1080, whose digits also add up to nine. The significance of the number 1080 was based on yin/intuitive properties as well as the radius of the moon. John Michell cites the 108 beads of the Hindu rosary, the 1080 pillars of Valhalla, and the "Holy Spirit" of Christianity as examples of the association of the number 1080 with the "feminine." Apparently the feminine principle throughout the ancient world was understood to be the lunar principle, the ubiquitous consort or sister-bride of the masculine sun. Since 801 contains the same digits as 1080, the dove was selected as an appropriate symbol for the goddess and was later adopted by Christians to represent the Holy Spirit (το αγιον πνευμα), whose sacred number, like that of the Earth Spirit (το γαιον πνευμα), is also 1080. So the Holy Spirit and the Earth Spirit are both linked by gematria to the lunar/feminine principle and to the dove.

And the number for the Greek word for "dove"—801—has a further degree of significance in Christian usage. In Greek, the value for alpha is 1, while the value for omega is 800. So the dove is equated by numerical association with the "Alpha and the Omega," an epithet of the "Holy One" who represents the eternal union of all opposites—the "beginning and the end," "the first and the last." This connection clarifies the identification of the dove with the Holy Spirit in Christianity, as well as some of its earlier, feminine associations.

Suddenly the descent of the dove of the Spirit upon Jesus at his baptism in the River Jordan is far more significant than we might at first have imagined. While it may have been the voice of God that was heard to proclaim Jesus as "my beloved son," as the Gospel of Mark records, it was the universal emblem of the Sophia/Holy Spirit, the 1080, that came to rest upon his shoulder. Symbolic interpretations like this one may have encouraged early Gnostic Christians to proclaim Jesus the child of Sophia, Holy Wisdom.

During the 1960s an ecumenical council met at the Vatican and formulated documents to instruct the Church. An interesting comment was circulated, derived from the deliberations of the council, one that, for too long it appears, has been ignored. In essence, it suggested that the bishops should listen to the people, because the Spirit of God "resides" or "rests" in the people. This assertion is a powerful reinforcement of the principle of the 1080—the Holy Spirit carried in the "sacred containers" or "earthen vessels" (2 Cor. 4:7)—the members of the human family. This is the definition of Church: she is the collective "bride" and sacred container in whom the Word of God (801—the Alpha and the Omega) is manifested by action of the Holy Spirit. Theologically speaking, the collective Church is the feminine partner of God, a metaphor derived from passages found in the prophetic books of Ezekiel and Isaiah in the Hebrew Bible where YHWH is the characterized as the bridegroom and Israel his bride.

CLUSTERS OF MEANING IN NUMBERS

One of the first contemporary books to look seriously at the subject of New Testament gematria was Del Washburn's 1977 volume entitled *Theomatics: God's Best-Kept Secret Revealed,* coauthored with American basketball star Jerry Lucas. Apparently Lucas met Washburn by accident at a seminar and was so enthralled with hearing about Washburn's research on numbers found in the Bible that he helped the mathematician to get his work published.[3] The book's title in Greek means "the mathematics of God," and the volume elucidates the gematria of the entire Greek New Testament.

What Washburn did was to assign to every letter in every word of the New Testament its numerical value based on the Greek numbering system and then, presumably with the help of a calculator and a computer, to add up the numerical value of every epithet, every phrase, and every verse of Christian Scripture. He discovered that the texts of the New Testament are full of what he calls "clusters"—numbers that are multiples of a basic concept expressed as a number. The use of case endings and the definite article enabled the authors of the Greek New Testament to manipulate their words so that their sums would correspond with significant numbers of the sacred canon within a margin of error of ± 2 (while in classical practice, the allowable error was ± 1). Washburn and Lucas were convinced when they wrote *Theomatics* that God alone was responsible for the messages thus hidden in the texts of Christian Scripture, but a wider reading of classical works indicates that the practice was not confined to the New Testament.

Washburn's work is an important resource, and many clusters he identified are extremely enlightening. Anyone who knows Greek letters can confirm by simple addition that the sum of the letters in the Greek spelling of the name Jesus (Ihsous) is 888. But why is that significant? One must dwell on the mystical aspects of the number for a moment to assimilate its full impact. Clearly the Greeks spelled the name of the sacrificed Jewish king differently from the phonetic "Yeshua" of his native Aramaic or Hebrew; their motive for their unique spelling of the name was its supercharged gematria, the triple 8.

Although the entire Old Testament, as we have noted, seems to be built around the sacred number seven, for the Christian community of the New Covenant, the number eight was of paramount importance. Because it follows the number seven, whose symbolic meaning is tied to the eternal cycles of days first set forth in Genesis and, by extension, all of time, eight was for Christians the number of the *new* day or New Age. Eight signifies regeneration; the resurrection of Jesus occurred on the "eighth day," the day following the Jewish Sabbath—literally, the "new day" of Christianity. Baptismal fonts are often octagonal to symbolize "new birth in Christ." The gematria of the name Jesus (Ihsous), 888, bears the meaning "the epitome of regeneration," the "dawn" or "sunrise" of the new age, and "resurrection." The values of the Greek letters in the entire verse "Behold a Virgin shall conceive" (Matt. 1:23) are designed to enhance this aspect of the Christ—their sum is 8880.

Another epithet belonging to this numerical cluster is "Lord of the Sabbath," a phrase that again adds up to 888. In Acts 20:7 we find: "On the first day of the week we were gathered together to break bread." The sum of the letters in this verse is 6216, which is the 888 (Jesus, "dawn of the new age") × 7 ("eternity, perfection, or completion"). These numbers illustrate the "cluster" theory of Washburn and Lucas and hint at further fascinating treasures in the New Testament that may be unlocked using the key of gematria. When they wrote their book, Lucas and Washburn were apparently unaware of the research of John Michell and other scholars in the fields of gematria and sacred geometry, and so did not interpret their own research in the light of the ancient cosmology.

According to John Michell, the number 444 was sacred for being the numerical equivalent of "flesh and blood"—the human condition. The letters of "the Word" found in John 1:14 add up to 444, reinforcing by gematria the meaning of the phrase "the Word was made flesh." The "lamb in the midst of the throne" (Rev. 7:17) equals 444 × 4 (an "epitome" of 4), and "the mediator, a man Christ Jesus," found in 1 Timothy 2:5, equals 4440. Amazingly, 4440 is also the product of the gematria for "Christos"—1480—multiplied by 3, confirming that the "Anointed One" is "flesh and blood," a human being chosen and anointed for a special mission of service. The historical Jesus embodies the highest example of the "earthen vessel," the human container of God's Spirit. This number 4440 is also related to 2220, a number that is equal by gematria to "the spirit of prophecy." The name of John the Baptist adds up to 2220 as well and is therefore also related by gematria quite appropriately to the Greek phrase "the spirit of prophecy." From these few examples provided in Michell's book *The Dimensions of Paradise*, we can begin to sense something significant occurring. The numbers associated with these familiar phrases from Scripture are a hidden treasure that as yet has barely been discussed by Scripture scholars.

Shall we continue to unravel number clusters found in the New Testament texts? The number 111 holds special significance as the foundation number (sometimes called the "master number") of all the triple "epitome" numbers—222, 333, 444, and so on. There are several ways that this "epitome" or "fullness" can be expressed. A number can be "epitomized" by its triple occurrence; thus, 222 is the epitome of "twoness"—duality or marriage. Since 4 is the number for Earth and the elements of the earth, 444 "flesh and blood" is the epitome of "fourness." The square or cube of a number can express the same idea, reemphasizing its meaning. In this way 7^3 (343) equates with wisdom and with Pallas Athene, goddess of wisdom, whose epithet "Pallas" has a value of 342.

It is believed that the names and sacred numbers of various gods and goddesses of the Greek pantheon were codified by about 500 B.C. The spellings were standardized to reflect the numerical values of their attributes. The mythology of Athene says that she sprang full-grown from the head of Zeus, a story that attests to her unique and superior mental capabilities. The geometry of the Parthenon—her temple crowning the hill above Athens—reflects the sacred numbers of Zeus (612), Hermes (353), and Apollo (1061), the Greek deities who represented intelligence, wit, and enlightenment, respectively.[4] By combining these specific measurements in the plan of the Parthenon, the architects honored wisdom in Athene, the embodiment of all mental faculties of reason, intuition, and acumen.

The numbers 7 and 12 representing "the Spirit and the Bride" are extremely significant in the Apocalypse of John, the final book of the canonical New Testament. Seven is the sum of 3 and 4, the first masculine and first feminine numbers, respectively, while 12 is their product. The book culminates with the nuptials of the masculine and feminine principles, heaven and earth, the Lord and the "New Jerusalem" arrayed in bridal splendor. The ratio 12/7 is roughly equal to the square root of 3, associated with the *vesica piscis*, a symbol formed by two circles whose circumferences pass through each other's centers and identified with the Holy Spirit. A *vesica piscis*—◊—with an altitude of 12 and a diameter of 7 illustrates the classic ratio represented by √3, a term that was unknown to the ancient geometers, although the generative properties of the figure were well appreciated. In Greek it was called the "matrix" and the "measure of the fish" and was considered one of the most important of all geometric shapes because it gave rise to so many other significant shapes in sacred geometry. Its generative powers are inherent in the Greek term *matrix* meaning "mother." In art, the shape is called the *mandorla*, a word derived from its almond (seed) shape, and as we noted earlier, the shape is the fundamental figure from which the "Seed of Life" mandala is derived.

In Revelation, the wall of Jerusalem, the Holy City, is 144 cubits (12^2), and the number of the elect is 144,000, numbers related to "the bride," η $\nu\nu\mu\phi\eta$ in Greek, which, by convention using the *colel* +2, has gematria of 144 × 7, while "Jerusalem" (*Ιερουσαλημ*) has a gematria of 864, or 144 × 6. Numerous fascinating clusters discovered by Del Washburn were apparently developed around these and other significant numbers found in the New Testament.[5]

THE 153 FISHES IN THE NET

How many readers of John's Gospel have wondered about the 153 fishes in the net mentioned in chapter 21? Were there really exactly 153 fishes? Did the seven disciples in the little boat out fishing on the Sea of Galilee who, following the instructions of Jesus to throw their nets on the starboard side, really stop to count them? The practice of gematria detailed by John Michell beautifully explains the significance of the number of fishes caught in the net. One of the Greek words for "fishes" (*ιχθνες*) has a value of 1224 or 153 × 8, and the word used for the "net" (*το δικτνον*) that is cast out to catch them also has a gematria value of 1224. The phrase "multitude of fishes" equals 153 × 16, and 16 is 4^2, which has strong associations with the 4's of Earth and the 444 of "flesh and blood" denoting the human condition. Thus, the "multitude of fishes" refers symbolically to the harvest of all humanity—the universal Church or Bride of Christ—those converted to his "Way."

The entire text of John 21 is based on the "fishes" and the "net." The association of Jesus (888) with the "new day" and the "fishes" (1224) seems to be an obvious, if esoteric, allusion to the New Age of Pisces just dawning at the exact time when the texts and tenets of Christianity were being formulated. The phrase "I am the Way" (John 14:6, εγω ειμι η οδος) has a gematria of 1225, or 1224 plus the *colel*, and "the way" equals 344 (7^3 + the *colel*), equating it with wisdom. John's Gospel is apparently alluding to the foundation of a new religion for the Age of Pisces of which Jesus is "the Way" and his apostles are the "fishermen" who gather the people (the harvest of fishes) into the unbroken net (the Christian community). The numbers enhance the message of the familiar text well beyond its literal meaning.

Every year, Christians celebrate the birth of Jesus on December 25. Although some have claimed that this date is associated with the winter solstice, the birth of the light, others have speculated that the choice of the date was influenced by the cult of Mithras whose birthday was celebrated on December 25. I suspect that the sacred numbers 1224 and 1225 may have been a contributing factor in the choice of this auspicious birth date for the "Divine Child" Jesus. Perhaps the numbers provided the rationale for the Christian "architects"—Church Fathers of the fourth century who designated midnight between the twenty-fourth and twenty-fifth day of the twelfth month as the exact moment of the birth of the Savior of the Age of the Fishes? Their reasoning is not recorded, but the numbers are certainly eloquent!

NEW LIGHT ON CHRISTIAN ORIGINS

Unlocking these secrets by means of gematria throws new light on the origins of Christianity and its fundamental tenets. The presence of gematria in the texts shows that the authors of the New Testament clearly had access to the combined knowledge of the sages and initiates—the astrologers, philosophers, and mathe-maticians—of the ancient world. They must also have recognized in Jesus, "the sacrificed king" of the Jewish nation, the archetype of the sun god—the Everlasting One—incarnate in the flesh. Marrying the Jewish ethical system and prophetic tradition with classical philosophy and cosmology, they made the risen Christ the focal point, or Kyrios, of the dawning New Age. The architects of the "New Covenant" deliberately formulated the teachings and "Good News" of the Anointed Christ (Messiah), casting the charis-matic scion of David in the role of Lord of the New Day. The cosmic mythos thus incarnated in Jesus of Nazareth, "the Word of God made flesh," sustained Western civilization through the crumbling of the classical world, through the barbarian onslaughts of the Dark Ages, and eventually into the modern era.

Perhaps it is time now to rearticulate the doctrines of the Christian faith in light of the enhanced meanings so long hidden in its own Scriptures. With renewed understanding, this body of doctrine could be transformed into an enlightened vessel able to reflect an ongoing human response to the Word and the will of the Spirit. With the help of this dynamic new understanding of the texts sacred to Christianity, we might heal the burned-out wasteland of the twentieth century and restore the balance nec-essary to maintain and nurture life on our blessed planet Earth.

> To you, O Lord, I cry,
> for fire has devoured the pastures of the plain,
> and flame has enkindled all the trees of the field.
> Even the beasts of the field cry out to you,
> for the streams of water are dried up,
> and fire has devoured the pastures of the plain.
>
> JOEL 1:19–20

4

ARCHITECTS OF THE CHRISTIAN FAITH

The authors of New Testament documents wrote in Koiné, the lingua franca, or common spoken Greek of the Roman Empire in the Near East. Although Jesus of Nazareth was a unique historical person, the religion we now call Christianity was not born in isolation. As we have noted, the Church fathers were part of a larger stream of scholars and sages educated in the esoteric traditions of Egyptian and Persian priests. Their studies included sacred geometry, astronomy, and philosophy. This connection of Christianity with earlier esoteric traditions can be deduced from studying the writings of classical philosophers, including the likes of the Greek sage Plato, an initiate of the Pythagorean school who also studied with Egyptian priests and Persian Magi.[1]

In the first century A.D., nearly one-third of the citizens of the Roman Empire were either Jewish or "Judaizers," that is, persons who were in sympathy with the monotheistic religion and high ethical code of the Jews. In the wake of the apostles' missionary journeys to the outlying reaches of the Empire, conversions to the Christian faith were numerous, not just among the poor and the oppressed, but even among the upper strata of Roman society, including many women. Converts from this educated elite were probably aware of the gematria evident in the writings of the New Testament and other first-century Christian documents.

Many of the leaders and patriarchs of the infant Church, including Paul, Origen, Clement of Alexandria, and later Augustine, converted to Christianity in midlife and brought to their study of the Hebrew Scriptures and Christian Gospels a highly structured foundation in classical philosophy. The earliest of these scholars, those who encountered Christian missionaries in the first century, were undoubtedly responsible for the mathematical system of gematria evident in the New Testament and other early Christian documents. Numerous examples are found in the epistles of Paul written to the Christian communities of the Roman Empire between A.D. 51 and 67, as well as in the Acts of the Apostles (A.D. 63–65), the four canonical Gospels (A.D. 70–95), and the Book of Revelation (c. A.D. 95–100).[2] While the practice was widespread, not every word in Greek has gematria that is relevant to the numbers of the canon of sacred geometry. Proper names, like those of the deities Zeus and Athene, and Ihsous (Jesus) and phrases that were deliberately "coined" are more apt to display significant sums than are words of common usage, whose spellings were not so contrived.

In the Gospels, Jesus is called *tekton*, a Greek word that meant not merely a carpenter skilled in making cabinets or furniture but a designer, construction engineer, or architect. A *tekton* could build a house, construct a bridge, or design a temple. Following in the footsteps of their Master Builder, early architects of the edifice of Christian theology formulated significant epithets and doctrines for the "Good News" and the "Way" of the infant faith community based on the cosmology already in place. Gematria was heavily employed by the author of the Book of Revelation, the final book of the official canon, in his account of his heavenly vision. We must examine some of the numbers found in this enigmatic book most probably written in the closing decade of the first century. The numbers convey hidden meaning and enable us to unravel secrets encoded in his prophetic insights.

THE NUMBERS 666 AND 1080

The most widely recognized of all esoteric numbers from the classical cosmology is at the same time one of the great enigmas encountered by devout readers of the New Testament. This mysterious number is declared to be the "number of the beast," 666. "Here is wisdom, let him that hath understanding count the number of the beast: for it is the number of a man; and his number is six hundred and sixty and six" (Rev. 13:18).

Scholars have offered numerous explanations for the phrase "the number of the beast." Of the many suggestions I have encountered, John Michell's brilliant interpretation is the most convincing.[3] In brief, Michell demonstrates that 666 is the number used throughout the ancient world to refer to the male/solar principle—the procreative power and positive energy of the cosmos—equivalent to the Taoist *yang* often described as "banners waving in the sun." This is the solar/masculine number, derived from the "magic square of the sun," a diagram wherein the number values from one to thirty-six are arranged in six rows of six numbers so that each row adds up to 111, recalling the powerful solar symbolism of the monad. The sum of the entire box is 666.

In its unmitigated extreme, the number 666 represents the exercise of raw, abusive power, the power of the tyrant. Crocodiles and Rome's Caesars provide good examples of the solar 666, as does Ba'al, the omnipotent "Lord and Master" and "Cloud-Rider" worshiped by Israel's Canaanite neighbors. In the Apocalypse, 666 is the number of the "beast with the ten horns." A horn reflects the archetype of the male triangle, synonymous with the "blade"—unmitigated power exercised without mercy. The "beast" is dissociated from his feminine counterpart and the feminine side of his own psyche. This beast, like the beast in the

6	32	3	34	35	1
7	11	27	28	8	30
19	14	16	15	23	24
18	20	22	21	17	13
25	29	10	9	26	12
36	5	33	4	2	31

Figure 4.1. *The magic square of the sun. The numbers from 1 to 36 are arranged so that each row (vertical, horizontal, and diagonal from corner to corner) adds up to 111, representing the "One"/Sun.*

book attributed to the Hebrew prophet Daniel, does not represent any one tyrant—the emperor Nero or Caligula or Adolf Hitler— but rather the power principle of tyranny itself. The raw power of the 666 principle can be appropriated by any totalitarian or repressive regime, from the historical empires of Egypt, Babylon, Assyria, and Rome or the power-drunk fascist and totalitarian regimes of the twentieth century, such as those led by Hitler and Stalin, to the repressive Taliban regime in Afghanistan and thugs in urban street gangs. Every authoritarian potentate and dictator embodies the solar principle, and the number 666 can be applied with equal justification to all of them. The distinguishing marks of a society that adulates the authoritarian 666 are a callous disregard for the poor, the powerless, the "little ones," and women. Such a community forms a power-oriented regime, at once violent, materialistic, and corrupt.

Hints from the literature and lore of the ancient world help us to grasp more fully the inherent meaning of the number 666.

In 2 Chronicles 9:13 it is recorded that the weight of the tribute money paid to King Solomon was "666 gold talents"—a fitting tribute to a powerful "solar" monarch. In his books on symbolic number, John Michell is careful to point out that the creative male principle is both necessary and good: the number 666, representing this solar energy (victory, power, authority, order, action, righteousness, obedience to law) is positive. But in the extreme, when not properly complemented with the feminine principle, it becomes both dangerous and destructive. One of the important secret numbers of the Pythagoreans was believed to be thirty-six, honored because the sum of each number added together in sequence from one to thirty-six equals 666, the symbolic equivalent of unadulterated, relentless "solar" power—the dominator, pure and simple.

As we have already seen, the power of the feminine manifested both in the Holy Spirit (το αγιον πνευμα) and its anagram, the Earth Spirit (το γαιον πνευμα), is assigned the lunar number 1080, which represents the complementary feminine principle. The "Holy Spirit" was considered feminine as reflected by the feminine gender of *ruach*, the Hebrew word for "spirit" or "breath." In Latin, the translation of Holy Spirit into "Spiritus Sanctus" took on a masculine form and connotation not found in Greek or Aramaic. So the Christian formulation of the Holy Spirit as the third person of an all-male Trinity, the "Spiritus Sanctus," caused the *ruach* of the Hebrew Scriptures (and of Jesus) to lose her feminine identity, although her attributes of life-giving waterbringer, comforter, and traveling companion (paraclete) remained feminine. Based on the radius of the moon, the feminine principle 1080 was lunar, the "sister" who mirrors the light of the masculine sun. Associated with the lunar influence on the movements of the oceans' tides, 1080 was also associated with the waters of the earth and with the "underground stream"—the intuitive and unconscious aspects of the feminine.

THE GRAIN OF MUSTARD SEED

One significant quotation, found at the heart of the entire Gospel teachings, is the reference of Jesus to the "reign of God" in the metaphor of the grain of mustard seed. In a parable that is almost certainly an authentic teaching of Jesus, he states, "the Kingdom of God is within you" (Luke 17:21) and compares this kingdom to the lowly seed of the mustard plant. A similar parable appears in all three of the synoptic Gospels: "The Kingdom of God is like a grain of mustard seed, which a farmer sowed in his garden. Although it is the smallest of seeds it grew into a tree with great branches and the birds came to nest in it" (Mark 4:30–32; parallels in Luke 13:18, Matt. 13:31)

This parable contains an astonishing hidden meaning that will enlighten all those "who have ears to hear." When Jesus used the image of the "grain of mustard seed" as the symbol for the kingdom of God, the powerful meaning of this image was encoded in the numerical value of the Greek phrase. Indeed, Jesus' pronouncement that "The kingdom of heaven is like a grain of mustard seed" may be among the most fundamental declarations in the entire Gospel. Remarkably, the sum of the letters of this cherished simile, the "grain of mustard seed" (κοκκος σιναπεως), is the number 1746. The profound esoteric revelation of this number calls out to be recognized, for it is the union or sum of the numbers 666 and 1080! In the ancient canon, the number 1746 represented the marriage of the opposites, the union of *sol* and *luna*, of the masculine and feminine. This same number is also the sacred number for "fusion," Plato's word for the union of the "Same and the Other." "Fusion," as Plato meant it, is best understood with reference to "the nuptials of the opposites," "the cosmic dance," or "integration" in the Jungian sense. The number 1746 represents the fertilized cosmic seed and is the number equivalent of the hieros gamos expressed as a hexagram, ✡.

According to this use of gematria in his teaching, Jesus actually proclaimed that the kingdom of heaven was the harmonious union of the opposing principles, the fusion of the lunar 1080 and the solar 666—the reconciliation or sacred union of the opposites.

The "grain of mustard seed" is not the only phrase in the Greek New Testament to bear the number 1746. According to John Michell's calculations, the list of New Testament epithets and phrases that bear the sacred number of fusion include, among others, "Emmanuel the son of Mary" (Matt. 1:23), "the Hidden Spirit," "the Universal Spirit," "Fruit of a vineyard" (Mark 12:2; Luke 20:10), "Jerusalem, the city of God," "precious pearl of Mary," and "offspring of a virgin's womb."[4] Believing that the numerical correspondence of all these significant Christian phrases was accidental on the part of the architects of the "New Covenant" would be preposterous. The number of fusion is demonstrably identified with "the Divine Child," the "wholeness" that is the fruit of sacred union.

Apparently the authors of the New Testament deliberately included these phrases in their texts to correspond with important symbolic numbers of classical antiquity. The only other explanation is that the numbers and phrases are mystically connected by the direct action of the Holy Spirit, the preferred explanation offered by Washburn and Lucas in *Theomatics*. These authors approached the New Testament gematria from a Christian theological viewpoint and were apparently unaware of the ancient canon of sacred number and the importance of numbers such as 1746 in the classical system. In any case, the numbers are enormously significant and have been too long ignored by exegetes of the New Testament.

I consider it very probable that Jesus himself, a rabbi of the Jewish faith and heir to its law and traditions, deliberately used Koiné phrases containing the sacred numbers now encoded in the Greek of the Gospels.[5] Modern scholarship suggests that the historical Jesus thought and spoke principally in Aramaic, but it seems clear that he also knew and spoke the Koiné of the Roman Empire. It cannot be accidental that the "grain of mustard seed" used as a metaphor for the "reign" or "kingdom" of heaven has the gematria of 1746, the sacred sum of wholeness or the nuptials, the number of the sacred union of the masculine and feminine energies. And it cannot be accidental that Jesus in all three of the synoptic Gospels used the mustard seed to illustrate his point about the reign of heaven, which is, according to its gematria, a domain of harmony and wholeness that accompanies the integration or "yoking" of the opposites. Jungian psychologists will immediately recognize and understand this harmony as the "integration" of Logos (reason) and Eros (relatedness). In Jungian terminology, harmonizing the opposing principles is the desired goal of each individual personality and spreads from each person out into the community, ultimately transforming the world. It is also found as a fundamental and cherished tenet of medieval alchemy—the *coniunctio* of the sun and moon, often depicted as the archetypal king and queen in intimate embrace.

HARMONIZING THE OPPOSING ENERGIES

In *The Dimensions of Paradise,* John Michell discusses the similarity of the diagrams and measurements of the ideal "New Jerusalem" described in Revelation, Stonehenge, and Saint Mary's Chapel at Glastonbury, a church built on the site of one of the earliest Christian churches in Western Europe.[6] All three temples, one in literature and the other two built on the ground in England, illustrate the same cosmology and relationships of measurements of the sacred canon. The inner circles of all three sacred sites have the same symbolic diameter (792), and each is surrounded by a square whose perimeter (3168) is the same as the circumference of the inner circle, a "squaring of the circle" that was a classic illustration of the harmonizing of the irrational and rational, of heaven and earth, masculine and feminine domains. In the interior of the circle Michell envisions a six-pointed star. This mandala—the archetypal "template" of the cosmic temple—represents the intimate union that brings peace, harmony, and well-being to the surrounding community and countryside. Since the purpose of building a temple was to harmonize the cosmic energies, invoking the power and attributes of a god or goddess and drawing them into the community, it is not surprising to find this principle applied to shrines and temples of antiquity, though the construction dates of Stonehenge and Glastonbury were separated by nearly two thousand years.

The Δ has long been equated with the masculine solar principle, and the complementary feminine ∇ represents the antidote, the refreshing water that ensures that the fire of the procreative, assertive masculine does not rage dangerously out of control. As we have seen, the feminine "water triangle" is associated with the lunar feminine aspects of 1080, including the workings of the Holy Spirit. One of the most significant Christian phrases coined to bear the number 1080 was πηγη σοφιας (fountain of wisdom), with all its connotations of the irrigating and refreshing streams of living water. It is precisely these waters that are dried up under the relentless rays of the solar principle characteristic of totalitarian government and fundamentalist religion. When the balance at the core is not achieved, the violence and ultimately holocaust inherent in the solar/fire triangle are the result.

As dangerous as the threat of conflagration inherent in the rampant male principle 666 is the unharnessed power of the feminine principle, the 1080. In its extreme it becomes the raging floodwaters of the irrational, anarchy, madness, a murky swamp, or a bottomless pit. Balance, thus lost or destroyed, needs to be reestablished according to the archetypal model for wholeness. The ✿ mandala—the sacred marriage of the 666 and the 1080—must be made conscious—taught, honored, and cherished—and allowed to illuminate us. Only in balance are the principles safe and life enhancing. When one is ascendant and the other neglected, as has happened globally over a period of several millennia, the entire society becomes warped and distorted. The sinister shadow of the repressed and neglected feminine—Eros denied!—now rears her ugly head in the dissociated, violent, and rebellious behavior of undisciplined youth, criminals, and terrorists. Scorned as bride and partner and denied a position of honor, she becomes a hideous Medusa lashing out to cause destruction to the fundamental institutions on which the human family relies: government, church, school, and family—civilization itself. This assessment of the fundamental crack in Western civilization appears to be simplistic, but we are dealing with the scorning of a powerful archetype—the bride—which has enormous consequences for a planet whose nations perennially honor male preferences and pursue policies oriented toward the exercise of power.

Violent aberrant behavior is often manifested by persons who suffered deprivation and abuse during childhood—a condition currently prevalent in the global family. Where is the tender concern of a nurturing mother for her offspring? In worshiping a god of power and might whose will is interpreted by a patriarchal hierarchy of powerful prelates, we are creating the very wasteland we fear, for according to esoteric wisdom, "as above, so below." What we worship, we become. We are creating the wasteland for which clear-cut forests, scarred mountainsides, dying species, and melting icecaps are but tragic examples. The abused children, the exploited laborers, the maimed veterans—and the planet herself—cry aloud for reprieve! Our civilization is reaping a bitter harvest of the bride denied. When the patriarchs of early Christianity supplanted the model of sacred marriage that was at the heart of the infant Church and denied Mary Magdalene as the consort of their sacrificed bridegroom/king, they could not have foreseen the tragic consequences of the broken mandala.

HEALING THE WASTELAND

In myths featuring a wounded or crippled king (or god), the wound is often to the foot or thigh, a common symbol for the genitals in Western art and literature. The wound of the king or god can be healed only when his lost feminine counterpart is restored. A novel by the British author Nevil Shute called *The Legacy* recounts the ancient theme of the wounded king and the wasteland starved for the waters of the sacred feminine. The book later became the movie *A Town Like Alice,* immortalizing the story of the sacrificed and resurrected bridegroom and his beloved as in the ancient mythology of the hieros gamos. Their reunion is the source of the blessing, joy, and fertility that spread into the surrounding community.

In the esoteric Hebrew tradition the Holy of Holies was understood to be the marriage chamber where the union of Yahweh with his counterpart, the Shekhinah, was consummated. With the destruction of the Temple of Jerusalem, so goes the Jewish myth, the covenant relationship of Yahweh and Shekhinah was disrupted. Yahweh returned to the heavens to reign alone, while his bride was forced to roam the earth in exile, like the community of Israel in Diaspora. The remnant of Israel, the devastated community, is depicted as the desolated widow Jerusalem in the Jewish apocalyptic books of Lamentations and Baruch, where the dark "Widow of Zion" is abandoned and distraught, the faces of her princes "born to the purple" now "black as soot" and "unrecognized in the streets" (Lam. 4:4–8). The Shekhinah, the immanence or "feminine" aspect of God, rests in the people of the community, and so shares the fate of Israel, the "daughter of Zion" represented by the dark bride, now widowed, abandoned, and reviled.

The same consort—the Shekhinah or sister-bride of Yahweh—is represented by the dark bride in the Song of Songs. This bride is described as "dark, but lovely," but her "swarthiness" is easily explained: She represents the devalued feminine—sunburned and dried out from serving the demanding solar principle, working in her brothers' vineyard (Song of Sol. 1:6). Her own vineyard she has neglected, a poignant statement of the sadly devalued condition of the feminine principle. Eventually, after a period of anguished separation, the bridal couple of the song is reunited in the orchard of pomegranates.

One particularly heartbreaking stanza of the Canticle refers to the sufferings of the bride desperately searching for her lost bridegroom in the city streets. The "guardians of the walls" encounter her wandering abroad in the city at night. These men beat her and strip away her cloak. As city guardians, the pillars of the patriarchal establishment, they cannot allow the woman to wander unprotected in the streets at night. For her own protection and for the safety of the community, she must be kept under strict control. This attitude toward women is manifested in certain strict fundamentalist religious communities today; often a woman is kept veiled and behind closed doors. She must be protected precisely because, having been systematically devalued, she is not revered as "sacred partner" but instead is denigrated and treated as an object. In these communities, a woman is not a sacred person but is a mere possession to be enjoyed at the whim of her male owner.

The Song of Songs was understood in antiquity to have been a wedding song of the archetypal bride and bridegroom. It was retained in the Hebrew Bible and later adopted by Christianity, where, in the earliest centuries, the dark bride of the Song was widely understood to represent Mary Magdalene—the acknowledged sister-counterpart of Jesus. She was understood to bear the archetype of the entire community as *ekklesia* (church).[7] In many songs and legends—including fairy tales like "Cinderella" and "Sleeping Beauty" and folklore of the world—the separated bridal couple is finally united, inevitably healing the symbolic wasteland caused by their distressed separation. This archetypal theme recurs by definition, appearing from generation to generation, since the separation of the partners representing the opposite energies constitutes the wounded condition that spawns the wasteland.

It appears that the Christians of the first centuries recognized the hieros gamos at the heart of the Gospels. The association of Christ with Tammuz, another bridegroom/god sacrificed in springtime rites, was recognized by Saint Jerome, who mentions in his writings that the cave in Bethlehem where Jesus was born was said to have been the birthplace also of Tammuz, the male consort of the goddess Ishtar in Babylonian mythology. This same "sacred bridegroom" was the fertility god for whom the women of Jerusalem were found weeping in the prophecy of Ezekiel (8:14). The fertility cult of Ishtar and Tammuz was widely popular throughout the Near East and even in Israel until prophets and priests of Judaism anathematized it. Parallels with the Christian celebration of the passion, death, and resurrection of Jesus described in the Gospels are obvious; in the Gospels, it is Jesus for whom the women of Jerusalem mourn. And preeminent among the women who mourn him is Mary Magdalene, "who was standing outside, weeping at the tomb" (John 20:11), a situation that parallels the ancient fertility rites of the sacrificed bridegroom/king in which the bride seeks the tomb of her deceased beloved and finds him resurrected in the garden.

CUSTODIANS OF THE ANCIENT TRADITION

The esoteric tradition of sacred number, geometry, and gematria was passed into Christianity through the mystery schools of the Hellenized world.[8] These schools were the repository of scholarship and mystical lore in classical times and well into the early Christian era. Through the mystical science of gematria, the secret wisdom of the ancient canon was incorporated into the New Testament. As we have seen, the formulators of Christian doctrine deliberately coined epithets for Jesus and key elements of his teachings so as to reflect by gematria the sacred dimensions of the cosmic Temple, itself a mirror of the perfect harmony of measurement and proportion of the created cosmos. The name "Lord Jesus Christ" *(Κυριος Ιησους Χριστος* in Greek) was deliberately created to obtain a sacred number reflecting the Spirit of the Age that encircles the universe and permeates creation—Plato's "World Soul." This number—3168—was fundamental to the dimensions of the New Jerusalem mandala articulated in the Book of Revelation and to the sacred temple at Stonehenge as well.[9]

Some of the early Christian fathers—most notably Tertullian, Hippolytus, and Irenaeus—were aware of gematria in New Testament texts and were evidently disturbed by it, since they wrote strong polemics against it, castigating Gnostic Christians for their use of numbers theology. There is evidence in *Against Heresies,* written by Irenaeus (c.130–200), that certain books and passages of the New Testament have an inner meaning that can be deciphered only by gematria. He harshly chastises Gnostics for their use of numerical analysis in interpreting Scripture. Hippolytus of Rome chastises Valentinus, a Gnostic teacher who preached a Christian doctrine that included the sacred union of the bridal chamber, accusing him of using the symbolic numerical system of the Pythagoreans as the basis for his teachings. For centuries scholars have puzzled over such pronouncements, at a loss to decipher their precise meaning and unable to piece together enough evidence to unlock for themselves these tantalizing enigmas of the Bible. Now at last we find the key; it lies in the gematria encoded into passages of the Greek New Testament. It was these same Gnostics whose numbers theology was derided and anathematized by the orthodox whose hidden library discovered at Nag Hammadi in the Egyptian desert shows that they honored Mary Magdalene as the consort of the Savior and his beloved. We will return to the theme of the lost bride in the final chapter but will first look at other important beliefs of the earliest authors of the Christian Scriptures encoded in the gematria of their texts.

5

THE SPIRIT
AND THE LAW

It appears that the original tenets of early Christians based on their memory of Jesus and his teachings were later distorted and altered by Church fathers converted to the new faith, who supplanted the teachings of the beloved rabbi with their own doctrines and dogmas. In this chapter we wish to examine the historical background of the ministry of Jesus and the community that surrounded him in Judea, the community of believers whose written accounts eventually became the sacred texts of Christianity. We will see how the gematria of some of these foundation texts can be used to enhance our understanding of certain important themes of the early Christian authors. Since the texts with which we are concerned were written in Greek, only the gematria of Greek phrases is relevant to this study, although, as will be noted occasionally, the same important values are found in Hebrew sacred texts as well.

Probably born in Athens, a prominent resident of the cosmopolitan Hellenized Egyptian city, Clement of Alexandria (c. 150–c. 215) was a Christian philosopher fascinated by the hidden knowledge he discerned in Christianity. He articulated the idea that his faith was a "new song"—the marriage or "harmonizing" of classical Greek philosophy based on reason with the prophetic tradition and high ethical awareness of Judaism. The roots of this idea are already available in the Gospels, the Acts of the Apostles, the epistles of Paul, John, and Peter, and the Apocalypse of the New Testament. These texts, written by various authors at different times, were copied often because of their importance to the infant Church and only much later compiled into an official body of texts called the "canon." Many other works sprang from the Christian community and were also honored and copied, but they were not accepted as canonical because they did not appear to have the authenticity or primacy of other texts. A prerequisite for selection of a Gospel into the canon was a strong tradition that the text was actually written by an apostle or eyewitness present during the earthly ministry of Jesus. But in spite of theories to the contrary, it is the consensus of Bible scholars that none of the Gospels was the work of an eyewitness who actually knew Jesus. And this has always been true of the epistles of Paul, who himself admits that he never saw Jesus and that he even brutally persecuted Christians prior to his famous conversion experience on the road to Damascus.

Because the New Testament begins with the Gospel of Matthew, we often overlook the fact that the earliest of the canonical texts are the epistles of Paul, followed by the Acts (c. 63–65), written by Luke, who is believed to have been a close associate of Paul's. This book describes the experiences of the apostles after the Crucifixion and the descent of the Holy Spirit in the form of tongues of fire that inspired them to venture forth to preach the "Good News" of Jesus Christ, the risen Lord. It also describes the conversion experience of Paul and his missionary journeys to encourage converts to the newly forming religion. The earliest Gospel written was that of Mark (c. 70), followed by those of Matthew, Luke, and John, in that order. Matthew's Gospel precedes Mark's in the canon because it includes the narrative of the birth of Jesus, a suitable starting point for the biographical account of the ministry of Lord. Mark's Gospel begins with the Baptism of Jesus in the River Jordan. Each author attempted to write a coherent story of Jesus and his sojourn among the people of Israel from available oral and possibly some written sources now lost—stories told and retold among the Christians who had known Jesus and honored his memory. Both Matthew and Luke borrowed heavily from Mark's earlier version of the story, adding embellishments of their own, while John's Gospel shows a strong mystical influence and contains certain elements that tie it closely to eyewitness accounts, especially in the details concerning the physical layout and features of Old Jerusalem and the events surrounding the Crucifixion. This gives an air of authenticity to his Gospel, but his account differs in significant ways from those of Mark, Matthew, and Luke, whose accounts are called the "synoptic Gospels" because the three authors seem to have "seen" in a similar way many events in the life and ministry of Jesus.

The epistles of Paul to various communities of early Christians were collected as a body of teachings and eventually included in the canon of the Christian Scripture. They express Paul's teachings, which in some ways seem to differ significantly from those attributed to Jesus in the Gospels. This seems particularly to be the case regarding his view of the efficacy and importance of the Jewish law, which Paul believed was superseded by the sacrificial death and resurrection of the Son of God, whom he expected to return in glory to establish a reign of God on Earth. According to Paul, certain fundamental tenets of Judaism could now be waived: one need not be circumcised; one need not marry; one need not obey the strict dietary restrictions found in the Jewish Torah. Paul's innovative teachings were designed to appeal to the Gentiles of the wider empire, but they left the many of the Jewish followers of Jesus aghast!

It is not controversial to suggest that the historical Jesus was an antiestablishment figure in his own time. In fact, it is clear from the Gospels that he was considered a revolutionary. To understand better the impact of his teachings, we need to understand the political scene in Palestine at the time of Jesus. The underlying realities of the period were devastatingly simple: Rome ruled. The fiercely independent and volatile Jewish people had been allowed certain privileges to worship their God as their law—the Torah—prescribed, and Rome was careful to allow the Jewish religious leaders, the Sadducees, a nominal position of authority, at least in religious matters. The Roman emperors also retained King Herod's heirs as tetrarchs of the province of Palestine. But that did nothing to endear them to the Jewish people. The Jews hated Herod's sons just as intensely as they had hated their brutal father.

POLITICS IN PALESTINE

Ruling Palestine at the beginning of the current era was a complicated affair. The Hasmonean rulers of Israel, descendants of the "freedom fighter" family of the Maccabees who had successfully wrested their country from the grip of Greek overlords, eventually became Hellenized and generally lax in the protection of the Jewish law. Having purified the Temple of Jerusalem in the second century, the ruling priestly family gradually resorted to petty squabbling and rivalries. Eventually they succumbed to the power plays of Herod, the warlord from Edom who made a deal with Rome enabling him to mount the throne of Israel. The Jewish people hated Herod for usurping the Holy City and throne of King David and did not forgive him, even though he married the beautiful Mariamne, a granddaughter of the last Hasmonean ruler Hyrcanus II, in an attempt to legitimize his claim to the throne.

Ruthless and evil, Herod the Great was an implacable tyrant whom history judges a monster. In successive power plays he murdered the surviving kin of his wife, including her teenaged brother whose legitimate royal lineage entitled him to the position of high priest. Mariamne, in the style of a true daughter of the Maccabbees, hated her cruel foreign husband with every fiber of her being. Finally, in a fit of rage, Herod ordered her murdered, and eventually he killed off her sons as well, thus wiping out the legitimate claimants to his throne and leaving his sons by several of his other four wives to divide the kingdom after his death in 4 B.C. He is also indicted in Matthew's Gospel for his massacre of the "innocents" in an attempt to snuff out the life of the infant savior prophesied by the Magi. Small wonder, with this history, that the Jewish people scorned and abhorred the scions of the king they dubbed "the Great Butcher." And small wonder perhaps that the next generation of mothers chose a name derived from that of the beloved Mariamne for their own daughters.

The perversions of the Herodians did not abate with the death of Herod. The Gospels tell us that John the Baptist was beheaded by the tetrarch Herod Antipas at the whim of his niece Salome. His wife Herodias had been angered by the prophet's condemnation of her illicit marriage to her husband's brother. She arranged for Salome to dance for Herod Antipas and then to request the head of the Baptist as a favor. Judaism had strict laws regarding the fidelity of women, and the people of Judea must have been outraged at the dissolute behavior of Herod and his surviving sons. The mere fact that these nominal kings collaborated with the hated Romans added fuel to the fire that smoldered in the hearts of the Jews. Rebellions were spawned and quickly squelched by the Roman legions garrisoned throughout Asia Minor, leaving the people of Judea in abject poverty and misery. Times were cruel, and the flickering hope for a national savior was tenderly fostered in their hearts from year to year, nurtured by prophets of impending apocalypse, the "Day of the Lord" when Yahweh would intervene with awesome wrath to restore freedom to his people and bring their enemies to justice.

The voice of John the Baptist crying in the wilderness, "Prepare the way of the Lord" was charged with emotional power. In great numbers the people flocked to be baptized by John—to be purified for the coming of the promised Messiah. They envisioned a savior who would save them from the cruel oppression of Roman rule and the ever-encroaching corruption of pagan influences.

RABBINIC JUDAISM

At the time of Jesus, Judaism had become enmeshed in a complicated network of rules and laws. Strict observance of dietary laws was required, along with mandatory participation in cultic rites of animal slaughter—prescribed purification rituals and sin offerings. A strong priesthood in the Temple controlled the religious life of the theocratic community, enforcing the commandments set forth in the Torah. The priesthood formed an elite class whose power was centered in the cult of animal sacrifice. During the early decades of the first century, the priestly families forming the ruling class of the Roman province of Palestine continued to exploit the poor. And, as they grew ever wealthier and more corrupt, blind to the plight of the miserable citizenry, various factions arose in opposition to their cultic priesthood.

These factions, disgusted with the politics of collaboration with the Romans, were eager to reform the religious life of the nation. Among these political factions were the Zealots and the community that authored the Dead Sea Scrolls found near Qumran. Both groups were anti-Roman religious reformers, who apparently had close ties with the early Christian community in Jerusalem. These groups comprised nationalists intent on overthrowing Roman hegemony by force of arms; they were radical freedom fighters and purists, who were "zealous for the law" and intensely patriotic.

Also in opposition to the elite Sadducees and the cult of the Temple there arose the rabbinical sect called the Pharisees. These teachers were interested in reforming and purifying the religious practice of Judaism. They studied the law as set forth in the Torah and interpreted the law as defining a relationship between God and each individual, teaching that God was present in each home and heart. The rabbis insisted that each person must be ritually pure in order to serve God in spirit and in truth. In Roman-occupied Palestine, they deplored the pagan influence on Jewish life and the defiled and corrupted Temple priesthood. The two parties, the Sadducees and the Pharisees, were at odds with one another during the several centuries of Rome's occupation of Jerusalem. Following the destruction of the Temple in A.D. 70, the Pharisees' interpretation of the law was able to survive in Diaspora, while the power of the priestly cult centered in animal sacrifice was irrevocably terminated when the Temple on Mount Zion was physically destroyed, its stones thrown off its walls one by one, smashing into the streets below. The day of this disaster, the ninth of Av, lives still in infamy and is marked by ritual commemorating the national humiliation of this catastrophe.

Rabbi Jesus

How does the itinerant rabbi Jesus fit into this scenario of political and religious factions in first-century Judea? One issue of great concern to the later followers of Jesus was how to reconcile his more radical teachings and attitudes recorded in the Gospels with Jewish law as stated in the Torah. This issue permeates the four canonical Gospels, most often in dialogues that Jesus conducts with the Pharisees. In the Gospel texts, these religious teachers accuse Jesus of disregard for certain aspects of the law of Moses. Like Christianity, the Pharisaical (Hasidic or Rabbinic) movement in first-century Palestine was an attempt to reform the religion of the Jews, perceived to be polluted after the long period of close contact with pagan cults of the Greek and Roman empires. In some of the Gospel texts Jesus disputes the interpretation of the law and the prophets given by the Pharisees and gives his own interpretation. In cases where the interpretation of

God's law was in question, Jesus often interprets strictly; in cases of man-made rules, he is considerably more lenient.

The Gospels relate that Jesus turned over the money changers' tables in the Temple during the Jewish spring festival of Passover, when, by law, Jews of all nations flocked to Jerusalem to offer their yearly sacrifices in the Temple. We can only imagine the scene that ensued: coins of all denominations from every outlying province rolling around on the floor of the Temple, while the people scrambled and scuffled with one another to retrieve them. Undoubtedly Roman troops were needed to quell the near riot ignited on that day. It is clear from the Gospels that the Sadducee priests were not inclined to support Jesus. They constituted a strong branch of the repressive establishment, and, according to the scriptural account, they cooperated with the Romans to arrest and sentence Jesus to death, most likely in an attempt to prevent the rebellion that was stirring among his followers and threatening to spread among the assembled pilgrims.

But the Pharisees, too, seem in the Gospels to be at odds with Jesus. In fact, the authors of the Gospels indicate that the Pharisees tried to set traps for Jesus and find excuses to repudiate his teachings. He taught his vision of the law with amazing authority and was far too clever for them, sometimes choosing a middle ground in their disputes, but more often interpreting their Scripture for them in a new light. "The Sabbath was made for man, not man for the Sabbath," he admonished (Mark 2:27). Clearly his teachings were a refreshing new understanding of the relationship of God to his people and his children to one another. "I came not to abolish but to fulfill the law," he claimed (Matt. 5:17). But at the same time, he gave it new life—a new dimension of spiritual awareness based on the fundamental law of Judaism: "You shall love the Lord your God with your whole mind and heart and soul . . . and you shall love your neighbor as yourself" (Matt. 22:37).

INTERPRETING THE LAW

The dualism between the spirit and the law was reconciled in Jesus. There was the law of Moses honored for over one thousand years—the law of the book. But there was also a higher law—that of the heart: "I desire mercy and not sacrifice" (Hos. 6:6). It was the spiritual law proclaimed by the prophets that required one to worship God in spirit and in truth, walking humbly while serving the poor, the orphaned, the widowed, and the foreigner. This was the fundamental tenet of the Gospel: "Whatever you do to one of these, the least of my brethren, you do unto me." In statements like these, Jesus declared the solidarity of God with the *anawim*— the "little poor" oppressed and scorned by the powerful elite.

Jesus did not repudiate the law, but when man-made rules conflicted with the demands of charity, he chose the latter, waiving dietary and Sabbath restrictions with daring impunity. He held a higher standard than the literal interpretation of the law: "There is nothing outside a man that, entering into him, can defile him; but the things that come out of a man, these are what defile a man" (Mark 7:15). Jesus thus declared all foods clean while condemning as unclean the evil thoughts, adultery, murder, theft, jealousy, pride, and blasphemy that come from within, "out of the heart of man" (Mark 7:20–23).

In numerous instances the teachings attributed to Jesus were at odds with current interpretation of the law. On one occasion he healed an invalid on the Sabbath (John 5:5–16), evoking the wrath of the Pharisees, and on another occasion he allowed his disciples to pick corn on the Sabbath in violation of the rules forbidding work on the Holy Day: "The Sabbath was made for man, not man for the Sabbath" (Mark 2:27). Often Jesus dissolved the bondage applied by the law. He repudiated the hypocrisy of the Pharisees who give only lip service to the law, insisting on outward displays of piety, but not living in accordance with God's mandate to love. "They bind together heavy and oppressive burdens and lay them on men's shoulders . . . all their works they do in order to be seen by men" (Matt. 23:4–5).

JESUS AND WOMEN

One of the most radical aspects of Jesus' ministry was his attitude toward women, whom he treated with utmost respect and compassion. And he was also accused of fraternizing with tax collectors and street people. He raised the daughter of Jairus from death and healed the woman with the flux who merely touched his robe, an example of the people's faith in him. In the Jewish community, a woman caught in adultery was condemned to death by stoning. But when the authorities brought such a woman to Jesus, condemned to death in accordance with their law, he was more merciful: "Let him who is without sin cast the first stone" (John 8:7).

In another instance, asked about the divorce laws in his time, Jesus maintained the strictest possible interpretation of the law, even in the face of current practice that at the time was very lax. While the law allowed a Jewish man to put aside his wife for even trivial misbehavior, Jesus insisted that even in the case of a wife's adultery, the marriage bond was sacred. To the Pharisees, he quotes Genesis: "a man shall leave his parents and cleave to his wife. And the two shall be one flesh. What God has joined together, let no man put asunder" (Matt. 19:9–12). Jesus further suggested that in a case of infidelity on the part of a wife, the cuckolded husband should remain celibate rather than repudiate his adulterous spouse, and that he should wait—as "a eunuch for the kingdom of heaven"—in this celibate state in hopes that his straying wife would return to the marriage covenant.[1] In the milieu of liberal divorce laws that favored men and allowed women few rights, this statement must have sounded outrageous. The model for this radical teaching was the prophet Hosea. Instructed to mirror God's passionate love for his faithless spouse—the covenant but apostate community of Israel—the prophet had been told to exhibit inexhaustible forbearance when confronted with the adulteries of his wife, the prostitute Gomer. Of course, since many people of the time, including the Pharisees, could not have accepted this radical suggestion, Jesus exhorts them: "Let him who can, accept this" (Matt. 19:12).

The Jews hated the sovereignty of Rome, but Jesus advised: "render to Caesar what is Caesar's and to God what is God's" (Matt. 22:21). Teachings like this must have disappointed those of his followers who sympathized with the nationalist factions. The people were suffering political oppression, yet Jesus said, "The kingdom of God is in your midst!" (Luke 17:21). These sayings of Jesus have a familiar ring for those who know the Gospels. We are so used to hearing them that we seldom stop to think that at the time when they were uttered many of them were surprising if not utterly radical! In fact, one of the standards Scripture scholars use to determine which of the statements attributed to Jesus in the Gospels are really authentic is to ask how radically the statement differs from the teachings and practices of his time. According to these scholars, the more radical the statement, the more likely that Jesus really said it.[2]

GEMATRIA AND THE LAW

Interestingly enough, the gematria of the phrases that have to do with the practice of the law throw a great deal of light on the entire issue of legalism—of goodness and evil, godliness and sinfulness. Let us allow these numbers to tell their story.

On the surface, it seems that the early Christian texts actually refute Jewish law. The cluster of numbers that refer to the law are multiples of 23. This number is related to other numbers having to do with the physical universe and the nature of man. The sum of 2 and 3 is 5, the number denoting well-being and physical human being (5 extremities, 5 senses, 5 digits on each hand and foot), while the product of 2 and 3 is 6, the number of the physical universe, which according to Genesis was created in six days. The gematria for "Adam" is 46 (23 × 2), and coincidentally, or by design, the number of chromosomes in a human being is also 46, 23 from each parent. This association with the human condition and the notion of sin and evil derived from the story of the fall of the first parents from grace may have inspired Augustine to formulate the Roman Catholic doctrine of "original sin," which states that everyone is born in a sinful state and requires that the stain of this sinful nature be washed away by the waters of baptism.

Washburn and Lucas point out that many references to evil are also derived from 23: for example, 23 × 12 is 276, the number on which references to Satan, Beelzebub, evil, the dragon, and Hell are built.[3] The Greek gematria of Satan, $\Sigma \alpha \tau \alpha \nu \alpha'$, is 276 × 2; "the evil one," $\tau \omega\ \pi o \nu \eta \rho \omega$, 276 × 8; while "the dragon," $\tau \omega \delta \rho \alpha \kappa o \nu \tau \iota'$, in Revelation 13:4 is 276 × 6. Washburn notes that the Hebrew quotation from Isaiah 14:12 "How art thou fallen from heaven, oh Lucifer, son of the morning" also yields the sum 276 × 6, which resolves to 9 as do so many of the important sacred numbers (666, 1746, 1080, 3168).

The number 276 is the number for the "law of Moses," and according to Washburn and Lucas, it is particularly prevalent in phrases found in Paul's epistles. The Greek words for "evil," "man," "corruptible," and "die" all bear the number 276 by gematria, linking them with the doctrine that "the wages of sin is death" (Rom. 6:23). Other significant numerical cognates of the number 276 calculated by Del Washburn are included in the following list of phrases:[4]

"in sin you were born" (John 8:34) = 276 × 6
"stone tablets" (2 Cor. 3:3) = 276 × 2
"the Sabbath Day" (Luke 13:14) = 276 × 8
"the first covenant" (Heb. 8:15) = 276 × 6
"curse of the law" (Gal. 3:10) = 276 × 5

"the letter killeth" (2 Cor. 3:6) = 276 × 4

"religion" (Acts 26:3) = 276 × 2

"The law is binding" (Rom. 7:1) = 276 × 5

"unclean" (Luke 4:33) = 276 × 2

"the righteousness of the scribes and Pharisees" (Matt. 5:20) = 276 × 18

"but where there is no law, neither is there transgression" (Rom. 4:15) = 276 × 11

From this list of New Testament phrases whose gematria is based on 23 × 12 (276), we have strong evidence that an important issue for the Christian authors of these documents was obedience to the law of Moses as articulated by the Jewish Torah and interpreted by the scribes of Judaism. According to most scholars, none of the Gospels was written in Jerusalem. The Gospel of Mark, the earliest, was probably written in Rome, for Roman converts (although some current research suggests Syria), and the others were written in outlying cities: Antioch, Alexandria, and Ephesus are considered likely locations. By the date when Mark's Gospel was written, probably A.D. 70–71, Jerusalem had been obliterated and its surviving populace widely dispersed. It probably seemed to the citizens of the Roman Empire that Yahweh had abandoned his covenant people and left the "community of the law" in shreds.

Under the influence of Paul, the early church had, by the time the Gospels were written, to some extent repudiated the Jewish law and formed a "new covenant" that was not based on the Torah and the Mishnah—teachings of the scribes and Pharisees—but on grace and belief in Jesus, the universal savior who had come to remove the "curse" or burden of the law. With the destruction of the Temple, some Christians even suggested that God's wrath had punished the Jews who had misunderstood Jesus and his teachings. Christian authors seem to have consolidated their position as separate from Judaism by concretizing an anti-Pharisee attitude in the Gospels, which is especially pronounced in certain passages of John's Gospel (written c. 90–95).[5]

As we saw on the list above, the epistles attributed to Paul are full of references to 276 and hint at the underlying issue that—for Paul—separated Christians from Jews in the latter half of the first century: the conflict between exoteric, "outward," or external practice of religion, and "esoteric" or interior spirituality. Jesus had seemed to preach the inner covenant—the commitment of the heart—and to repudiate the elaborate outward displays of religion practiced by the scribes and Pharisees: "Woe to you teachers of the law and Pharisees, you hypocrites! You give a tenth of your spices—mint, dill and cumin. But you have neglected the more important matters of the law—justice, mercy and faithfulness. You should have practiced the latter without neglecting the former" (Luke 11:42). Pray and do penance in secret, he had counseled them, and your heavenly father will reward you in secret. In the Gospel version of the story, Jesus calls the Pharisees "whitewashed sepulchres"—beautiful on the outside, but full of corruption (Matt. 23:27).

THE CRACKED VESSEL

During the first few decades of Christianity, converts in Jerusalem under the conservative leadership of the apostle Peter and James, to whom Scripture refers as the "brother of Jesus," insisted on strict observance of the Jewish law, while the Gentile converts of Paul, residing in cities of the empire far removed from Jerusalem, chose the way of freedom from that law. The proper interpretation and practice of the law became a fundamental source of friction among the early Christian communities of the Near East.

The Acts of the Apostles, written about A.D. 63–65, recounts tension between Paul's interpretation of the mission of Jesus and that understood by James and Peter, who were not at all happy with the zealous missionary work of the new, self-proclaimed apostle Paul. The convert-apostle's mission was to the Gentiles of the Empire, but his preaching to them set him at odds with the more conservative Jewish leaders of the early Church still centered around the Temple in Jerusalem.

There seems to be a significant break here. Somehow, between the teachings of Jesus quoted in the Gospels and the preaching found in the epistles of Paul and other early patriarchs, something seems to have gone radically askew. Jesus is quoted as having said that he came not to destroy the law but to fulfill it (Matt. 5:17). He seems to have been fully conscious of his prophetic mission within Judaism. In his teachings recorded in the earliest Gospel, Jesus does not repudiate the law of Moses or the teaching of the prophets. He only attempts to waive or to soften the man-written interpretations of those rules that had evolved gradually into a heavy burden on the people, destroying the spirit that lives behind the literal interpretation of the word of God.

From the study of the gematria clusters of 23 × 12 found predominantly in the epistles, we can surmise that the thrust by Christians to separate themselves from the law of Moses and the "first covenant" did not necessarily stem from the original teaching of Jesus. Interpretations of the mission and message of Jesus were not cast in concrete from the beginning, but were gradually evolved, under the influence of Gnostic and especially Docetic doctrines (which denied the flesh-and-blood humanity of Jesus and emphasized his spiritual nature and divinity), finally culminating in the separation of Christianity from the Jewish synagogue in the closing decades of the first century. Certain fundamental doctrines of the Christian communities, especially their repudiation of the law of Moses, along with their gradually evolving doctrine of Jesus as the incarnation of the "rising sun" of the New Age, were unacceptable to the leaders of the reformed rabbinical Judaism that survived in Diaspora after the fall of the Temple. Christianity was gradually repudiated by the rabbis of the first century, and the two movements, begun in the crucible of

Roman-occupied Judea as sister factions in opposition to the corruption of the Temple priesthood, went their separate ways.

One interesting question becomes important: where would Jesus himself have fit into the institutions that evolved after his death on the cross? After all, the people in the streets of Jerusalem had hailed him as their king and messiah, the long-awaited son of David. Alternative Gospel-based versions of the Christian Way derived directly from the traditions of early Christian communities with "low Christology" struggled to survive in later centuries. Within two generations, principles of gender equality and other important teachings of Jesus were subverted and an "elevated Christology" attributing divinity to Jesus and equating him with God the Father emerged. Paul's teaching of the Second Coming superseded the assurance of Jesus that the reign of God was already within us, waiting to be celebrated as the wedding feast of sacred partnership. The parable Jesus told of the king who invited guests to celebrate the marriage banquet of his son sums up the story: The invited guest repudiated the invitation to embrace the "sacred marriage" model with its inherent gender equality that was the radical foundation myth of Christianity.

Was Paul himself one of the leaders of the early Church who hijacked the teachings of Jesus and set them on a course of his own design? This question is being examined by a growing number of scholars. It is clear from the Book of Acts that the family and friends of Jesus were not in sympathy with Paul's claim to be an apostle nor with his assertions about the teachings of Jesus. He seemed to be forming a new religion based on his own highly individual perception of the "risen Lord" which was immediately at odds with the leadership of the Christian followers of Jesus in Jerusalem. The Gospels had not yet been written, but the stories of Jesus and his ministry were being circulated at the time of Paul's missionary journeys. Paul did not quote the teachings of the rabbi Yeshua, but rather preached his own theology of salvation in the name of Jesus, the crucified and resurrected Son of God.

There is no doubt that Paul practiced gematria; it occurs often in his letters, and not by accident. Because gematria is calculated and contrived by those who coin the phrases, it expresses their own agendas and prejudices, and Paul's use of the number cognates to enhance his teachings and support his position is very much in evidence. The question remains, where would Jesus have stood on the positions that Paul took in opposition to the other Christian leaders? Jesus might have maintained a more conservative position than Paul suggests, since the Gospel maintains that Jesus came not to destroy the law, but to fulfill it: "Therefore whoever does away with one of these least commandments, and so teaches men, shall be called least in the kingdom of heaven" (Matt. 5:19). Might this passage from the '80's stand in opposition to the teachings of Paul that were being spread throughout the pagan reaches of Rome's empire? Paul admits that he did not receive his teaching about virginity from the Lord (1 Cor. 7:25) but is only stating his own opinion. We are left to wonder if he preached his own opinion on any other occasions. It is apparent that the Jerusalem leadership thought so.

Jesus was crucified by Roman officers at the command of Pontius Pilate, the Roman governor of Judea. He suffered a death usually reserved for criminals and insurrectionists because the Roman authorities and Jewish High Priests perceived him to be a political threat. Yet Paul characterizes Jesus as the "paschal Lamb"—a sin offering reconciling the people to God. Jesus did not think of himself as the Lamb. He called himself the "Good Shepherd" and the "Bridegroom." He characterized himself as "servant of all"—not Lord of the Universe. He was "rabbi" to his friends, not "Kyrios." And on Easter morning when he encountered Mary Magdalene at his tomb, he requested her to go to his brothers and tell them, "I ascend to my Father and your Father, to my God and your God" (John 20:17). When the people sought to make him king, Jesus fled to the mountains. And when Peter wanted to build a "booth" to honor Jesus on top of the mountain where the "transfiguration" had occurred, Jesus rejected the suggestion. The idea that he would be claimed to be divine, born of the Father before all ages and of one essence with God, as expressed in the Nicene Creed, would have doubtless appalled the Jewish rabbi Jesus who walked in sandals along the dusty roads of Judea preaching a way of peace and reconciliation and compassionate concern for the poor. How did the early Church ever make the transition from this very human Jesus healing and comforting his countrymen in the villages of his homeland to the one we find in the celestial throne room of God in the final book of the New Testament, the Apocalypse of John?

We turn now to that book to discover what we can of its secrets long embedded in the Greek phrases of the apocalyptic vision. With the help of the sacred canon of number, a powerful new interpretation of Revelation beckons to us in chapter 7. The gematria in its passages provide an enlightening view of early Christianity and its relationship to Judaism, while casting new light on the "partnership paradigm" in teachings attributed to Jesus himself. It is time to unravel the mystery of the "nuptials of the Lamb," but we must first, in our next chapter, ascertain the background and agenda of the author of the Apocalypse in order to put his revelations into their proper context.

6

THE APOCALYPSE
AGENDA

Our discussion has so far centered around the sacred canon of number and the discovery that the archetypal design of early Christian churches reflects a knowledge of the same system of number correspondences found in the temples of the ancient world. Clearly, if this thesis is true, it indicates a strong continuity between the initiates of the Hellenistic mystery schools, the religions of the Roman Empire, and the early architects of the new covenant of the Christian faith. This established, it is time to examine in detail the final book of the New Testament, which reveals details about the cosmic dimensions of the New Jerusalem.

Of all the books of the New Testament, Revelation is probably the most enigmatic and misunderstood, its meaning and intent hidden behind a veil of obscurity. In the next chapter we will examine the gematria of certain phrases and words that unlocks secrets long hidden in this late-first-century Judaic-Christian text, casting new light on the fundamental teachings of Jesus encoded by the apocalyptic visionary who calls himself John. In this chapter the discussion will provide background about the agenda and worldview of the author-visionary, "John the Divine," and the context of the widely misunderstood prophecy in Revelation.

We have already studied the sad condition of the Jewish people whose leaders were puppets and collaborators with the occupying forces of Rome. The Jews deeply resented the brutal and repressive policies of the Roman overlords, and their expectations of a Davidic Messiah were whipped into a fever during the first century. They longed for YHWH to intervene on their behalf, to initiate the "Day of the Lord" described in Zechariah 14, and they prayed for the vindication of their people and the defeat of their enemies. This mind-set is encouraged in the epistles of Paul, who proclaimed the imminent return of Jesus to establish his kingdom on earth.

LIFTING THE VEIL

The word *apocalypse* comes to us from the Greek and means "lifting the veil," which calls forth an image of peeking behind a curtain, or perhaps the veil of a woman. The Apocalypse of John is not an isolated piece of writing but is one of many examples of this genre popular during the "inter-Testamental" period at the "turn of the Age"—at precisely the time when Jesus of Nazareth lived. The final book of the New Testament was only one in a long stream of prophetic writings that belong to the genre of apocalyptic literature that envisions the end of the Age. Visionaries of the Roman Empire prophesied cataclysms they expected to bring down the wrath of God upon the world's corrupt rulers and bring about the salvation of the oppressed. Since our present era—coinciding with the precessional end of the Piscean Age and the beginning of the Aquarian—seems to spawn similar hopes and fears, the vision described in the Apocalypse is tremendously evocative at this time.

The Hebrew prophet Daniel describes receiving a vision of the Son of Man and the Ancient of Days, and, long before Daniel, the prophet Isaiah was taken up to heaven to see the throne of God and had his lips cleansed with a burning coal (Isa. 6). Other Jewish writings of this apocalyptic genre include the Book of Enoch and the Testament of the Patriarchs, apocryphal writings that were widely circulated in the cities of Rome's empire at approximately the time when the New Testament texts were being written. Scholars who truly want to understand New Testament documents often study the contents of the widely popular Book of Enoch, which profoundly influenced the followers of Jesus.

Study of the genre of apocalyptic literature indicates that the vision of John found in the New Testament was part of a larger stream of Jewish and classical writings concerned with the end times. These prophetic works provided a glimpse into a future when evil would finally be destroyed and justice and goodness would be victorious in the cosmic battle. It is no surprise to New Testament readers that citizens of Judea in the first century A.D. believed that the end of the current age was imminent. Paul preached the immediate cataclysmic end of the age in writings that predate the written Gospels, so this violent demise of contemporary civilization is assumed by biblical scholars to have been a commonly held belief of the infant Christian church. In Mark's and Matthew's Gospels, Jesus himself prophesied that Jerusalem would fall and that her people would flee to the mountains to save their lives, but, since most scholars agree that these texts were written after the event, they may be a reflection of the known disaster that befell the Holy City and her people.

HISTORICAL BACKGROUND OF JOHN'S APOCALYPSE

Puzzling passages of the Apocalypse of John have defied interpretation for centuries. The book recounts a journey by its narrator under the guidance of a spirit or angelic companion. He is taken to the throne of God where he witnesses eschatological events that vindicate the righteous elect and punish their oppressors. In the work, Jesus, the Lamb, is seated at the right hand of the throne of God, reigning with God over the final events of the age. The throne of the Almighty (*Pantokrator*) is surrounded by the 144 thousands of the "elect"—the chosen servants of God—and the angelic hosts who sing praise to God and to his faithful servant, the Lamb.

The Apocalypse is a Judaic-Christian work, both poetic and prophetic; it contains mythological beasts and bizarre cataclysms—disasters orchestrated by a wrathful Deity to punish the wicked—elements the Book of Revelation holds in common with other apocalyptic writings of the era. Its powerful and disturbing images affect us, stirring deep emotions. The Apocalypse of John is a book of prophecy, and scholars agree that the book does not give accurate details of church or world history, nor does it prophesy a calendar of precise future events. With its bizarre imagery and enigmatic symbolism, it confounds simple interpretation; attempts to pin down its symbolic images to specific historical or geographical details have proved speculative and inconclusive. But thanks to modern scholarship and calculators, some of its hidden meaning has recently been unlocked using the key of gematria.

It is best to try to understand this book in the context of its own era. Comparison with other works of the period—Jewish apocalyptic texts, letters of the Christian patriarchs, and contemporary historical evidence—yields the consensus that the Apocalypse was written toward the end of the reign of the Roman emperor Domitian (A.D. 81–96), probably in about 95. Paul's teaching had led the first generation of Christians to believe that Christ's return to rescue them and usher them into his kingdom was imminent. When their expectations of this *parousia* were not met, they gradually revised their teachings to emphasize a beautiful and blessed life-after-life united with their Lord in God's heavenly realm. Subsequent generations, faced with brutal persecution and even martyrdom, derived considerable strength and comfort from these doctrines. But in the first century the Christian message was not yet cast in stone, nothing was doctrinal, and tradition had not yet been established. During this period, Christian communities were expelled from the Jewish synagogues of the Diaspora and were no longer protected by the special privileges allowed to the Jewish communities since the time of Herod the Great, who had negotiated privileges allowing the Jews to practice their own religion without having to participate in the civil religion and the cult of emperor worship practiced throughout the Roman Empire. Instead of being seen as a branch or sect of Judaism, the Christian believers were ultimately alienated from their Jewish roots during the decades at the end of the century and forced to set out on their own to form independent communities.

From the beginning, antagonism between the Jewish and Christian communities was theological, especially the articulation of the divinity of Jesus. Numerous persecutions were carried out against the Christians by the Jewish authorities in Jerusalem, as recorded in the Acts and Paul's early epistles. Some of the early Christians—followers of James, the brother of Jesus who was the first leader of the community in Jerusalem—continued to remain faithful to the Torah and the Temple worship for several decades until the destruction of the Temple in A.D. 70. But following the fall of Jerusalem, the Jews of Palestine were forced to migrate to other cities of the Empire and begin life anew as strangers in foreign lands.

Scholars suggest that the Gospels were based on "pericopes," a rich oral tradition of stories about Jesus' life and teachings that had been preserved by the original faith community. After the fall of Jerusalem, differing versions of these stories were retained in the widely scattered communities, and some of the most important sayings of Jesus may have been recorded in documents now lost.[1] Various stories and parables of Jesus were emphasized based on the individual needs and interests of each Christian community. It is to be expected that occasional embellishment and development of particular stories occurred before they were committed to papyrus, which explains why the texts of the four Gospels, while similar in many respects, differ greatly in others and have numerous contradictions. Both Matthew and Luke include genealogies of the ancestors of Jesus in their Gospel narratives, but they do not match. Luke mentions the shepherds to whom the angel announced the birth of Jesus, while Matthew tells of the visiting Magi from the east and the slaughter of the innocents by Herod. Mark fails to mention any of the birth narratives, beginning his Gospel with the baptism of Jesus by John the Baptist. Different details are emphasized in the various Gospels attesting to the diversity of the communities that honored the memory of the Risen Lord. We see this diversity of the early Christians reflected in Paul's epistles to the various cities and in the letters to the seven cities in the first and second chapters of the Book of Revelation.

THE ISSUE OF CHRISTOLOGY

The rival prophetic traditions of rabbinical Judaism and Christianity, both rooted in the teachings of the Hebrew prophets, were competing for authority in Asia Minor at the close of the first century. Christians claimed that Jesus was the culmination and fulfillment of Jewish prophecy and used Gospel passages to illustrate the point, believing that Judaism had been superseded by the new "Way" of their Lord. The underlying issue that separated the sibling faiths was Christology—the articulation of the true nature of Jesus Christ. Questions of Christology address a related series of issues: To what extent was Jesus of Nazareth a normal human being as opposed to an incarnation of a deity (similar to the Greek gods with whom the citizens of the Hellenized Roman Empire were familiar)? Was Jesus a god? Or was he an "earthen vessel" filled with the Holy Spirit of God? Was he a Son of Man, or a Son of God? Was he the son of Mary? Was he also son of Joseph, as is stated in the genealogies in the Gospels of Matthew and Luke? What does "Son of Man" mean? What did Jesus mean when he said he was the Son of Man? What did the Roman centurion mean when he said that Jesus was surely the Son of God (Matt. 27:54)? The divinity of Jesus was expressed in various ways by the diverse communities of first-century Christians—from belief in a fully human Jesus at one end of the spectrum to Docetic belief that Jesus was a pure spirit whose body was a mere illusion at the other end.[2] The First Epistle of John explicitly warns against the latter view, insisting that Jesus came "in the flesh" (1 John 4:2).

Questions about the true identity of Jesus first arose while he was ministering to the poor and the sick in the streets of Palestine, working miracles in God's name, and they have been with us ever since. "Who do people say that I am?" Jesus asks his apostles. "Some say Elijah, others say John the Baptist" was the apostles' reply. When pressed for his own view, Peter replies that Jesus is the Messiah, son of the living God (Matt. 16:16). But the beliefs of Christians about the identity of Jesus were not formulated overnight. They were the result of decades and finally centuries of Christian experience and revelation, struggle, and soul-searching. Christians of the "Johannine" community, centered around the Gospel teachings of the fourth Gospel traditionally attributed to the apostle John, equated Jesus with the "Word of God" (Logos) and developed a relatively "high Christology."[3] They considered themselves more enlightened than those Christians who followed the apostolic tradition of James and Peter, who had a comparatively "low Christology," denying that Jesus and God were one and the same being. For these "Jerusalem" Christians, there was only one God, the Holy One of Israel, the God of Jacob and Moses. Disciples of the apostles in the Jerusalem community regarded their Hellenized brethren with apprehension; they perceived them as idolaters. The closer one remained to Jewish roots, the less likely one was to share the high Christology of the so-called Johannine school.

Nor did the Judaic-Christians adopt the literal interpretation of the prologue of the Fourth Gospel that declared Jesus preexistent and equal to God. Later Docetic and some Gnostic heretics who derived their teachings from this same high Christology actually proclaimed the divinity of Jesus while virtually denying his humanity, a position denounced in the Apocalypse of John where the narrative deliberately stresses the human genealogy of Jesus—calling him the "Lion of the tribe of Judah" and the "root of David." In so doing, the author of the Apocalypse explicitly emphasizes the actual *human* origins and historical ancestry of Jesus, enabling us to characterize the author of the vision as promulgating low Christology.

Based on this discrepancy in Christology, what can we ascertain about the author of the final book of the New Testament? It is clear that he was intensely Jewish, steeped in Hebrew Scriptures, Old Testament linguistic patterns, symbolic numbers, and evocative images. He makes frequent allusions to verses from the Hebrew prophets, particularly Isaiah, Daniel, and Ezekiel, and his theology reflects the low Christology of the original Jerusalem Christian community. Although he writes in Greek, he thinks in Hebrew, or more likely Aramaic—a conclusion drawn from the syntax of the text and the numerous "Hebraisms" that stem from his frequent allusions to Hebrew Bible passages. The rudimentary Greek of the book is sprinkled with occasional barbarisms and awkward syntax, additional evidence that it was not the primary language of the author. Making deductions from these linguistic considerations, exegetes of Scripture consider it virtually certain that the author of the Apocalypse is not the same John who wrote the Fourth Gospel ("John the Evangelist") in spite of the name they apparently share.

The Apocalypse is probably the most thoroughly Jewish of all the books included in the New Testament canon. Its author belongs to the strong prophetic-apocalyptic tradition of Asia Minor. In the entire work, among countless epithets chosen, the author never attributes absolute divinity to Jesus, nor does he ever equate Jesus with God. He is a devout follower of Jesus, but fundamentally Jewish in his roots and outlook, a fact that accounts for the low Christology found in this final work of the New Testament canon. Because he writes in Greek, the gematria found in his book is based on the Greek alphabet, but the meaning of the values was a convention applied universally.

Jesus, the Servant of God

From the very first chapter, the author of Apocalypse characterizes Jesus as a "servant of God," calling him the "faithful witness, first born from the dead and ruler of the kings of the earth" (Rev. 1:4). This is a clear allusion to Psalm 89, where God chooses and anoints David, describing the king of Israel in these words: "He will call out to me 'You are my Father, my God, the Rock, my Savior.' I will also appoint him my firstborn, the most exalted of the kings of the earth . . . I will establish his line forever, his throne as long as the heavens endure" (Ps. 89:26–29). This passage is distinctly "adoptionist" in tone: the king is the chosen or anointed of God, but not equal to God. There is nothing in this prophetic passage from Psalm 89 that echoes the Platonic (Gnostic) flavor of the hymn found in the prologue of John's Gospel: "In the beginning was the Word, and the Word was with God and the Word was God" (John 1:1). Clearly these passages come from widely different traditions—one Jewish, the other Greek.

Apparently the Jewish author of Apocalypse believes Jesus to have been the promised Davidic Messiah, the slaughtered Lamb whom God has raised, but *not* a deity. God is the Almighty One who sits upon the eternal throne, who lives forever and ever, who created all things, "who was and is and is to come" (Rev. 1:8). The Lamb who sits at his right hand is clearly distinct from God, though "worthy of praise and honor and glory and power" (Rev. 5:13). Jesus, the Lamb, is "worthy to open the seven seals of the scroll"

(Rev. 5:5) that initiates the terrifying events of the Apocalypse.

Whenever the visionary tries to fall down and worship his companion, he is enjoined to "worship God." The term *theos*—"god" in Greek—is never applied to Jesus in this book. While God is referred to by the name *pantokrator* ("almighty") nine times in the text, the term is never applied to Jesus. Clearly the Jewish author of Apocalypse does not ascribe absolute equality with God to Jesus, nor does he embrace the high Christology of the Johannine community. The visionary of the Apocalypse encoded in his work the belief that it is wrong to attribute equality with God, the Almighty One, to his human "anointed" servant and lamb, the historical person Jesus. Numerous ancient texts were written by authors who used a pseudonym to increase the prestige attached to their work, and this appears to be the case here. The choice of the name "John" by the staunchly Jewish author would thus be an ironic twist, since the compelling visionary experience of *this* John actually attempts to correct what he believes is the distorted high Christology of certain Christians who in his view have been misled by the *other* John—the Evangelist—in *his* theological interpretation of the nature of Jesus.

The whole agenda of the Apocalypse is an apparent attempt to articulate the true nature and meaning of Jesus—Jewish prophet, priest, and king—and to warn of the danger of elevating the historical human Jesus to equality with the unseen God "behind the veil." Jesus is the "Chosen One"—God's anointed, and he is the Davidic Messiah proclaimed by the Hebrew prophets. In the Hebrew context he is both Lion of Judah and Lamb of God, but he is neither *theos* nor *pantokrator*, epithets that the author of the book reserves exclusively for God.

Speculation as to what motivated the author of the visionary verses has occupied Bible scholars for centuries. Was he merely encouraging persecuted Christians of Asia Minor to persevere in loyalty to Jesus, believing that God would come in power to punish their oppressors and avenge the wrongs perpetrated against the community of the faithful? The ultimate vindication of the righteous was a common motif throughout the entire genre of Jewish apocalyptic writings. In Revelation, the elect or chosen ones who remained loyal to God would be saved after the ravages of seven seals, seven trumpets, and seven bowls and their accompanying series of woes and plagues. Possibly the crisis that evoked the visitation of the wrath of God envisioned by the author of Apocalypse was a decree by the emperor Domitian demanding that he be worshiped as "our Lord and God" by the citizens of the Roman Empire, a decree abhorrent to Jews and Christians alike. Surely the appalling arrogance of the emperor would attract the lightning-wrath of God like a tall tree in a storm!

But other motives for writing this apocalypse can be discerned. The two greatest threats to the Christian churches of the first century were the erosion of zeal and the danger of believing erroneous or heterodox teachings. Since the formation of doctrines concerning Jesus Christ was still fluid at this time, diverse aberrant teachings were circulating, and in his epistles Paul himself records other frictions and factions causing divisions among the first generations of Christians.

Some scholars believe that the polemic found in the Apocalypse of John was directed against the influences of certain Docetic and libertine heresies that were eroding the Christian message in Asia Minor during the final decade of the first century. The teachings of some of these early Christian sects were attacked by the Church fathers because they tempted adherents to ignore the Ten Commandments—the law given to Moses—and to adopt the pagan morality of the Roman Empire. Some of the converts to Christianity had no understanding of the law of the Torah and the code of ethics that underlay Judaism. The practice of some of these unorthodox Christian groups took on characteristics of the mystery religions of the era, practices that often included sexual promiscuity and orgies. Clearly the patriarchs of the early Church felt compelled to take a firm stand against such behaviors.

After the fall of Jerusalem and the death of the first-generation witnesses to the ministry of Jesus, there was no one who could claim to have absolute authority to interpret Christian doctrine. With no central authority, diverse communities of Christians struggled with the interpretation of the life and teachings of Jesus and arrived at varying answers.

Even before the destruction of the Temple, Paul had presented a unique challenge to the Christian leaders because he claimed to have received his knowledge of the risen Christ through direct revelation in a vision instead of having walked personally with Jesus during his ministry in Palestine. As we have mentioned, Paul's teachings were often at variance with the more conservative views of James and Peter. The three men had several serious quarrels concerning the practice of certain Jewish laws—specifically those concerning the circumcision of Gentile male converts and the consumption of unclean foods. Eventually such issues were resolved, and after the dissolution of the Christian community in Jerusalem following the fall of the Holy City in A.D. 70, Paul's teachings ultimately prevailed.

DOCETIC INFLUENCES ON CHRISTIANITY

One tendency found among some sects of early Gentile Christians was to emphasize the deity of Jesus to the neglect of his humanity, denying physical flesh-and-blood functions. Their teachings existed side by side with those of other sects in Asia Minor who insisted on the full humanity of Jesus, and who believed that any articulation of the divinity of Jesus as equal to God was blasphemous. The latter considered the worship of the human person, Jesus, to be idolatrous, in direct disobedience to the first commandment given to Moses: "I am the Lord thy God. Thou shalt have no other gods before me!"

The author of the First Epistle of John refutes the Docetic denial of the human person, Jesus: "Every spirit that confesses that

Jesus Christ has come in the flesh is of God" (1 John 4:2). Early Christians were also in possession of copies of Paul's letter to the Romans, written in A.D. 57–58, and understood its reference to people who worship "an image made like corruptible man" (Rom. 1:23). The text of this epistle gives a list of the evils bred by idolatry—the worshiping of a created image—instead of the creator: "For this cause God has given them up to shameful lusts . . . being filled with all iniquity, malice, immorality, avarice, wickedness, . . . envy, murder, contention, deceit, malignity, being whisperers, detractors, hateful to God, irreverent, proud, haughty, plotters of evil, disobedient to parents, foolish, dissolute, without affection, without fidelity, without mercy" (Rom. 1:24–31).

The author of the Apocalypse of John fears the idolatry inherent in the worhip of Jesus found among his contemporary Christians who emphasized the divinity of Jesus and denied his full humanity. His own Jewish roots caused the mystic "John" to recoil from the worship of any image of God and from attributing anthropomorphic masculine aspects to the unseen ineffable Holy One, since the attribution warps and distorts the value system of the society formed in that falsified image. For that explicit reason the Jews had always been warned by their prophets to abhor worship of any idol or image of God: "You shall not carve idols for yourselves in the shape of anything in the sky above or the earth below or in the waters beneath the earth; you shall not bow down before them or worship them" (Exod. 20:4–5).

I believe that the Apocalypse is an attempt by the visionary to warn his Christian brethren that the idolatrous worship of the visibly masculine solar/power principle embodied in the Risen Christ will cause disasters to be poured out upon the earth. Whether the worship is offered to the Roman emperor or to the crucified king of the Jews, according to the visionary John, it is in both cases idolatrous because it substitutes a created image of God for the ultimate "Unseen Reality"—the Holy One hidden behind the veil.

7

GEMATRIA IN THE APOCALYPSE OF JOHN

There is ample internal evidence for interpretation of the Apocalypse of the New Testament along the lines discussed in the last chapter: the low Christology of the author and his conservative fear of what he perceives to be the consequences of the idolatrous worship of the Christ. Scripture scholars note that the central issue in the book is power, and its most compelling image is the throne of God.[1] In keeping with many mythologies of the East, the Holy One is portrayed as a potentate or "sun god," an awesome and omnipotent Supreme Deity who rules forever. In the Apocalypse, the Lamb of God is depicted with seven horns and seven eyes—all-powerful and all-seeing. Heaven is seen as a royal court, similar to that in the other apocalyptic writings of the period. The prophet Isaiah described his heavenly vision with these words: "I saw the Lord seated on a high and lofty throne, with the train of his garment filling the temple" (Isa. 6:1). In the Apocalypse, God is enthroned in unapproachable light; his appearance sparkles like jasper and carnelian (Rev. 4:20). His throne is surrounded by a halo as brilliant as an emerald; it emits flashes of light and peals of thunder. In the first chapter of the

Book of Revelation, Jesus is described in terms reminiscent of the "Son of Man" in Daniel 7 and 1 Enoch: he has eyes like a fiery flame, feet like burnished bronze, hair as white as wool or snow, a mouth with a two-edged sword, a face like the shining sun.

This portrayal of God and of Jesus in terms of an Eastern solar deity is dangerous, for it is apparent that what we honor we emulate. The "Almighty One" of the Apocalypse is the archetype of domination and judgmental sovereignty. He has little in common with the loving father Jesus tried to reveal to his compatriots in Palestine, the kindly parent who sustains the flight of sparrows (Matt. 10:29) and counts the hairs on our heads, nor with the Jesus who counseled us to love our neighbors and to wish even our enemies well. The New Testament image of this patriarchal and controlling Lord of heaven and earth has served to extend male domination during the entire two thousand years of Christian hegemony in Western civilization. Imaging God as omnipotent and male and associating the historical human Jesus with this same image constitutes a powerful idolatry, severely warping consciousness in favor of the eternal male solar/power principle. As a direct corollary of this distortion, the feminine principle has been scorned and neglected for two millennia.

NEW LIGHT ON THE APOCALYPSE

For most readers the secrets of the Book of Revelation have remained so far obscure. But, as the work of John Michell suggests, these secrets are hidden in symbols and in numbers sprinkled throughout the text, and their meaning can be deciphered by applying the number values of gematria to certain phrases of John's vision. We have already seen that the number 1080 represents the feminine—the realm of intuition, mystery, darkness, and passivity—while 666 represents reason, law, authority, and the generative power of the male, the power of the emperor and the genius of the scientist or sage. The sum of these two, their "nuptials," was 1746, the number by gematria of the "grain of mustard seed."

In the Apocalypse, the beast with the seven heads and ten horns (Rev. 17:3) is an embodiment of the male power principle 666. In his vision the author saw the end result of the masculine solar power or Logos orientation that eventually culminates in holocaust if it is carried to its technological extremes. The number 666 expresses positive energy. The principle is not evil in itself but becomes so only when it is honored or worshiped to the exclusion of its complementary principle, the 1080 of the feminine. The number of the beast represents the brutal and domineering bully who exploits and intimidates the children of God.

Worship of the sun principle was widespread in the Middle East. When great military empires of the area supplanted the old matrilineal fertility-oriented agricultural communities of the Neolithic period, they imposed state religions with a powerful priesthood celebrating an omnipotent god, of whom the Oriental despot with his fawning court was a mirror image. Ancient examples of this solar deity are Marduk, Zeus, Apollo, Mithras, Sol Invictus, and, according to the imagery in the Book of Revelation, even the Almighty God of Israel who, although he allows no images, sits upon the eternal throne of heaven surrounded by flashes of lightning and claps of thunder. He is "Lord of Hosts" and "God of Power and Might." All the nations of earth seem to be involved in this worship of raw power and the sun. Yet Jesus taught the opposite. He called his "father in heaven" Abba, which means "Daddy" in Hebrew. He showed deep concern for the *anawim* and preached a gospel of reconciliation. His "Way" was the way of Eros/relationship and illumination of the heart. The "Way" (οδος in Greek) has a gematria of 344—the cube of 7 plus the *colel* +1—linking it to Pallas Athene and Holy Wisdom herself.

THE IMPERIAL PARADIGM

When the power principle is honored as supreme, and its partner in consequence devalued, the feminine becomes a whore, bound in service to the solar principle. The community that is seduced and submits to the power principle 666, worshiping and serving the empowered male principle, is characterized in Apocalypse as the harlot who rides the beast—the phallic Δ. She represents the community or nation (or even the religious institution) that submits to the tyranny of a dictator instead of joining the resistance and fighting to be rid of him. The monstrous tyranny of political, military, and economic power is historically evident in the empires of Egypt, Assyria, Babylon, Greece, and Rome, along with numerous more modern empires and dictatorships we could mention. This totalitarian empire, wherever it manifests itself, is on an inevitable path of confrontation with the sovereign power of God.

And the wrath of God is poured out in answer. The author of Revelation noted the cataclysms of the first century—the earthquakes that destroyed Laodicea in A.D. 60–61; the destruction of Rome by fire in A.D. 64; the fall of Jerusalem to Roman legions in A.D. 70; the eruption of Vesuvius that utterly destroyed Pompeii in A.D. 79; and the grain famine in A.D. 92, so devastating that the Roman emperor Domitian decreed the reduction of acreage of vineyards to allow an increase in grain yield for the starving citizens of his empire. The author, along with other Jewish apocalyptic fundamentalists of the period, understands all of these natural disasters to be concrete proof that God is angry, perhaps like the God in the Genesis story who saw the behavior of Noah's contemporaries and was sorry he had made them. The *pantokrator* is lashing out to punish the sinful inhabitants of Earth. As if the sufferings brought about by cataclysm were not enough, the war and strife caused by the megalomania of the ruling class breed famine and pestilence—the ravages of the four horsemen of the Apocalypse (Rev. 6).

The poor and the disenfranchised cry out for mercy and justice against the forces of tyranny and oppression. These themes are universal in the apocalyptic writings of the period, including many texts found among the Dead Sea Scrolls at Qumran, and are also reflected in Paul's epistles to the infant Christian communities of Gentile converts in the Roman Empire. The apocalyptic fear and expectation reached a crescendo with the fall of Jerusalem's Temple and the final destruction of the hope of the Jewish nation at Masada in A.D. 73. Those Jews who survived sought refuge in other cities of Asia Minor, and their laments for their lost Jerusalem are poignant. Only gradually did Christians realize that their Lord Jesus did not intend to return to physically rescue his followers from the harsh reality of their earthly surroundings.

THE SECRET TRADITIONS

As we have noted, the esoteric tradition of sacred number, geometry, and gematria of the Hellenized Roman Empire was deliberately passed into the "new wineskins" of Christian teachings and writings. Presumably initiates of the mystery schools had access to a vast repository of knowledge, and by means of the hidden codes of gematria, the sacred tenets of the ancient canon were deliberately incorporated into Christianity. The architects of institutional Christianity understood themselves to be heirs in the continuum of the philosophical and mystical traditions of classical antiquity.[2]

In his books dealing with gematria, John Michell illustrates that many enigmas of the Apocalypse can be understood by means of gematria, while numerous verses can be totally misunderstood without this secret key. One example of this is found in the quotation "I am the Alpha and the Omega." This epithet, "the Alpha and the Omega," adds up to 2220, specifically identifying it with "the spirit of prophecy" (το πνευμα προφητειας) and "Christbearer" (Χριστοφορος) both of which have the same gematria. According to

Michell, 2220 is also the gematria of John the Baptist, Ἰωαννης Βαπτιστης, another "bearer" or "vessel" of the "spirit of prophecy."[3] In Revelation 19:10 the angel guide tells the visionary very explicitly: "Worship God. For the testimony of Jesus is the spirit of prophecy." It appears that the author of the book is portraying Jesus as a vessel of prophecy—a "faithful son" and servant of God. Several times in the Apocalypse the angel repeats the admonishment: "Worship God!" Any Jew faithful to the law would consider the elevation of Jesus to equality with God an unforgivable blasphemy, since their God permitted no physical form or images but was pure Spirit, undifferentiated Oneness or Holiness; the words *holy* and *whole* are derived from the same root word. To call a man—any man—"God" was anathema to the Jewish community in the first century of the current era. It still is.

The prophetic warning at the heart of the Apocalypse insists that the raising of the human Jesus to an object of cultic worship, as an image of an all-powerful and wrathful God of Justice, Power, and Might, is itself a deification of the solar 666, the male power principle: "This calls for wisdom. If anyone has understanding, let him calculate the number of the beast, for it is the number of a man, *and his number is 666*" (Rev. 13:18). John Michell added up the gematria of the phrase "and his number is 666" and discovered that the sum of its letters is 2368, the same sum as the Greek letters for the name of the man in question—"Jesus Christ—Ἰησους Χριστος."[4]

This discovery packs a shocking and powerful punch. It is bound to rock the boat—"Peter's bark"—sending theologians scrambling for an explanation. How could the author of the Apocalypse ever have meant to identify Jesus, the Christian Savior, with the dreaded Beast of the Apocalypse? For a Christian, the mere suggestion is blasphemous.

But the author of the Apocalypse was not a contemporary Christian. He was a first-century follower of Jesus, the crucified charismatic teacher and healer. And the author had intensely Jewish roots that caused him to fear that the high Christological teachings of his day were not only idolatrous but would inevitably bring the wrath of God down upon the entire community! The internal evidence of gematria encoded in this passage of the Apocalypse indicates that the idolatry that is the object of the visionary's dire warnings is the worship of "a man" who died "but is alive again" (Rev. 17:18)—not Domitian, the Roman emperor, but *the man Jesus*, the crucified king of the Jewish people.

With the interpretive insights provided by gematria, the purpose of the author of the Apocalypse becomes obvious. He seems to believe that the message of Jesus, the bearer of the "spirit of prophecy," is being corrupted into the cult worship of an idol—a human being declared to be equal to God—in a scenario no different from the imperial cults of Rome's Caesars, except that it is far more dangerous because it is archetypal, being celestial and eternal rather than earthly, illustrated by the esoteric principle "as above, so below." The visionary intuits this appalling danger when he sees the havoc wrought by the four horsemen and the plagues unleashed upon the earth.

In his epistle to the Romans (A.D. 63), Saint Paul had already warned the Christians against idolatry a full generation before the author of the Apocalypse (A.D. 95): "for while professing to be wise, they have become fools, and they have changed the glory of the incorruptible God for an image made like to corruptible man . . ." (Rom. 1:22–23). But certain communities of Christians had not understood how Paul's warnings could possibly apply also to the development of their own high Christology—honoring Jesus as God. In the Apocalypse, the scarlet-clad harlot who rides the beast is the symbol of such idolaters, seduced by the material and physical. This image stands for any community that worships a created form in place of the one true God who is Pure Spirit, the undifferentiated Holy One, an indictment, that would include Babylon and Rome and every other city on Earth that worships the solar principle embodied in a male image of God as the eternal Victor, Ruler, and Judge.

The ultimate end of this idolatry of a dominant male principle (the phallic fire-triangle Δ), as envisioned by the author of Apocalypse, is holocaust; for what we sow, we reap. It was no surprise to learn that the number 666 is intimately related to the occult "square of the sun," for it is nothing more than the solar principle expressed as a number. The number 1, the monad, as we have noted, represented "The One" (God) and the sun. The extreme or epitome of 1, 111, occurs in many cognates in the gematria of both Greek and Hebrew sacred texts. The Hebrew phrase "YHWH God" (Gen. 3:9) bears the sum 111, and the gematria of the declaration "I am YHWH your God" (Exod. 6:7) is 111 × 2, as is the phrase "YHWH God most high" (Gen. 14:22). In the prophetic Book of Daniel we find "Blessed be the name of God for ever and ever" (Dan. 2:20) which yields Hebrew gematria of 1110, the same sum that is found in the Greek phrase "the name of the Son" (1 John 5:13), while the "Name of Christ" (1 Pet. 4:14) is 2220, like the "spirit of prophecy" and the name of John the Baptist already mentioned. Another interesting cognate of 111 is found in 1 Timothy 2:5: "the mediator, a man, Christ Jesus" has gematria of 4440, reflecting the "flesh and blood" humanity of Jesus.[5]

Because six, as we have noted, represents physical creation, 111 multiplied by six yields 666, the equivalent of "solar power manifested on a physical plane." On an individual level, serving the solar principle causes "burnout." On a larger scale, it yields lethal high-tech weapons and ultimately—holocaust. The warning is inherent in the Apocalypse of John. Our Earth now reaps the terrifying harvest of the 666 orientation of the major monotheistic religions and their systematic denigration of the complementary feminine principle designed to sheath the sword.

NUMERICAL COGNATES OF 666

Numerous phrases in the New Testament add up to cognates of 666.[6] For example "wrath of God" (Col. 3:6) bears the value of 666, as does "great wrath" in Revelation 12:12. "The men who bore the mark" equals 666 × 9, according to Del Washburn's calculations in *Theomatics*, while the phrase "Those who had received the mark of the beast" equals 666 × 3. Other verses are associated with the number of the beast: "Those who worship the beast and its image" (666 × 6) and "Whoever receives the mark of its name" (666 × 6). It seems that the author of Revelation, in order to emphasize his point, went to great lengths to ensure that phrases describing the nature of the beast added up to cognates of the universally accepted solar number 666—harbinger of the seared wasteland lamented by the prophet Joel and, ultimately, of conflagration.

It is interesting to note that the Greek word for "wonders" (τερασιν, 665) found in 2 Thessalonians 2:9 also reflects the 666, as does the phrase "wrath of God" (οργη θεου, 667) used in Paul's letter to the Colossians—another example of total power! In other New Testament texts, wonders are signs of the Antichrist or beast: "According to the operation of Satan with all power and signs and wonders" (2 Thess. 2:9) totals 666 × 6. The Antichrist is also linked with 666: "The man of sin, the son of perdition" (2 Thess. 2:3) equals 666 × 6. And, not too surprisingly, "merchants of the earth" (Rev. 18:3) also bears the number for "power"—666. The intent of the authors of these Christian epistles seems to be to alert the hearer of the Word to the dangers of the unadulterated power principle rampant in the first century (and rampant still). Paul and the other authors of the texts, each with his own interpreta- tion of the "good news" of Christ's life, death, and resurrection, understood the principles of the canon of number and employed gematria to reflect these principles in their writings. But it was left to the author of the Apocalypse to take the implications of 666 to its ultimate extreme—highlighting the idolatrous worship of the man whose number was 2368 in place of the Unseen Holy One. Worship God alone!

It is the domination of the male principle enthroned in celes- tial glory in the mythologies and doctrines of the institutional religions—the highly charged, competitive rule by sword and by the "law of the jungle"—that becomes a devastating curse on the planet. Operating in harmony with its complementary feminine opposite, as it was in the hieros gamos mythologies of the ancient civilizations, the solar/masculine principle represented by the number 666 would be tamed and rendered benevolent; but without its partner, the *yang* orientation is dangerous—like power exercised without mercy. Ideally, the two principles yoked together should contain one another in a harmonious equilibrium.

THE MARRIAGE SUPPER OF THE LAMB

After the devastation of the wars, famines, and plagues detailed in John's Apocalypse, the marriage supper of the Lamb (Rev. 21) ultimately brings about the reconciliation of heaven and earth. The final chapter of the work is considered to be a late addition to the original text and is thought spurious and even heretical by some Christian scholars. But others believe that all of the books in the surviving canon of the New Testament are a gift of God, so perhaps we should take some time to examine the hidden meaning of these chapters even if they are, as some think, a late addition to the original work.

When the solar principle embodied in Jesus, "the Logos made flesh" (John 1:1), is brought into union with its feminine counterpart, "the bride," the result is the Holy City that has no temple and needs no light—for God is the Temple and Jesus is the lamp. Streams of water flow from the celestial throne, nurturing fruitful trees. The nuptials of the Lamb found in the final chapter of the Apocalypse produce the fulfillment of the ancient promise: "the desert shall bloom."

The principle of nuptials or harmonizing of the opposites in the sacred marriage celebrates the end of dualism and separation, prophesied so long ago by the prophet Isaiah: "No longer will you be called 'abandoned' or your land 'desolate,' for you shall be called 'beloved' and your land 'espoused'" (Isa. 62:4). The remnant of Israel, the community of the chosen, is traditionally depicted as the desolated widow Jerusalem in Jewish apocalyptic literature—as in the Books of Lamentations and Baruch found in the Old Testament. Now arrayed like a bride, this woman—"Zion"—is symbolically married to the male principle embodied in Jesus, bringing-about the reconciliation of the opposites, heaven and earth, male and female, spirit and flesh. The spiritual challenge of our time is to effect a reconciliation with the feminine—a bringing-about of the wedding of the masculine and the feminine to realize the *anthropos,* which can be described as a "perfected" or fully integrated human being.[7] This new harmony or "wholeness" will be celebrated in the New Jerusalem where streams of water flow out from the throne of the invisible God. The Spirit and the bride invite all humanity to come: "May all who thirst drink freely from the Water of Life" (Rev. 22:17). The eternal bridegroom and his nuptials with the bride in Revelation reflect the hieros gamos union of Jesus and Mary Magdalene implied in the Gospel stories of the anointing, death, and reunion of the beloveds. In his recent work *The Gospel of Mary Magdalene,* the French scholar-mystic Jean-Yves Leloupe comments that the male-female alliance in the final chapter of Revelation echoes the couple Jesus and Mary Magdalene symbolizing the twofold teaching of the Sophia and Logos. For those who have eyes to see, as well as ears to hear, "the world is still being illumined by the brilliance of Yeshua and Miriam."[8]

The gematria of the bride and the elect, or chosen community, is shown by Washburn and Lucas in *Theomatics* to share clusters of 144 (12 × 12), the number for "fullness" or "completeness" on the earthly or physical plane.[9] The number twelve is rich in associations of completion because it is the union by multiplication of 3, the first masculine integer, and 4, the first feminine integer. It is also understood to have associations with "flesh and blood" because it is composed of three fours (4 + 4 + 4 = 12). The other union of the numbers three and four—their sum, seven—represents eternity and perfection, "completion" as related to the passage of time and spiritual rather than earthly things as we established in chapter 2 when discussing the time cycles related to seven, the week, the sabbatical year and the jubilee year, and also the numerical attributes of Wisdom/Sophia, Pallas Athene, and the Holy Spirit. Addition is a linear function, as in measurements of time—for example, from here to eternity—while multiplication creates the square measurements on a material plane. So, as 7^2 is the completion of "a week of weeks" (forty-nine days), the number 12^2 represents completion or wholeness in the sense of something material, tangible, and visible, as in "the entire community," and "the perfect city." The mandala of the New Jerusalem in John's vision contains numerous overt examples of twelves: in the twelve apostles, twelve gates of the Holy City, twelve precious jewels; but also of sevens in the seven trumpets, seven bowls, and seven plagues that mark the passage of time.

According to the work of Lucas and Washburn, other New Testament cognates of the number 144 include the Greek letters found in "Jerusalem" (864 = 144 × 6), "the flock," "gather the wheat," the "endurance of the saints," and "marriage feast for the son." The exoteric geometry of the New Jerusalem is based on the number twelve—the twelve tribes of Israel and the twelve original Jewish apostles of Jesus help to form the model for the Holy City. The union of the Bride and the Lamb is at the center—the hieros gamos forming the nucleus for the twelvefold pattern emanating from their union—the union of spirit (7) and flesh (12)—that is the source of blessing and harmony for the whole planet.

Interestingly enough, Michell correlates the gemstones of the gates with the signs of the zodiac.[10] This point emphasizes the syncretism and interrelatedness of religion and philosophy in the milieu of the author of the Apocalypse. By the time the Apocalypse was written, in the closing years of the first century, the wife of Jesus had already been lost for a period of nearly sixty years—her whereabouts relegated to myth and legend, probably for her own protection, a theory developed in *The Woman with the Alabaster Jar*.[11] Second- and third-generation Christians in the Eastern Churches, born after the fall of Jerusalem, had no inkling of legends placing her in France; they believed her final resting place was in Ephesus with Mary the mother of Jesus, whom tradition places there in the custody of the evangelist John. Other kinfolk of Jesus, including his brother James, were perceived as threats to Roman authority and were martyred by the minions of Rome. By the end of the first century, the vision perceived by the author of the Apocalypse centered around a heavenly intervention and solution superimposed on the devastated earthly community—salvation coming out of the sky reminiscent of the deus ex machina of Greek tragedy.

The Book of Revelation has had a history of being acclaimed by some churchmen and repudiated by others. Justin Martyr of Ephesus (c. 135) believed the book to be apostolic in origin, and others of the Church fathers used it as Scripture, notably Clement of Alexandria (d. 215). Marcion (d. 160) rejected the apostolic origin of the book and discredited its canonicity, and Eusebius (260–340) agreed. Cyril of Jerusalem (313–386) excluded it from the canon altogether. Centuries later, John Calvin declined to write commentary on the Book of Revelation and Martin Luther believed of the text that Jesus was "neither taught nor known" in it, although he later modified this early position. There seems to be good reason for the reservations of these Christians exegetes concerning the book, considering that it was written by a Jewish-Christian convert and reflects the low Christology of his conservative Jewish faith: there is no God but God!

Because several influential Church fathers—Tertullian, Hippolytus of Rome, and Irenaeus of Lyons—deliberately stigmatized gematria found in the writings of the New Testament and discouraged the faithful from concerning themselves with the numbers in their Scriptures, the memory of the meanings of the numbers was eventually lost. It is fortuitous that the Book of Revelation survived the censure of the early fathers of the second and third centuries and can now be subjected to renewed scrutiny, yielding its hidden, encoded message to an age equipped with computers which facilitate the research cross referencing the gematria of its phrases and correlating their uncanny and enlightening correspondences.

THE ISSUE OF IDOLATRY

From the tablets given to Moses comes the voice of God, breaking the stillness with his thundering command: "I am the Lord thy God. Thou shalt have no other gods before me!" Throughout the history of their special covenant with God, the besetting sin of Israel was always idolatry, often portrayed, as we have noted, as harlotry—imaged in the woman riding the beast in the Apocalypse of John. The Hebrew prophets Ezekiel and Hosea also used the image of the harlot to represent the collective unfaithfulness of the chosen people to their covenant with God (Ezek. 16; Hos. 2 and 3). It is precisely the idolatry practiced by some factions of the Christian community that the Judaic-Christian author of Apocalypse both fears and abhors. Worship of the unbridled male principle is a great evil—not because it offends God but because it is so exceedingly dangerous. Such worship distorts society, causing the entire cosmos to be out of balance; this idealizing and idolizing of the male preference of the "son" allows domination of the earth by the active/solar male principle, which ultimately creates the wasteland. Only the nuptials of the Lamb, that is, the restoration of the feminine as his bride, can restore that harmony. All the ills of war, famine, and pestilence result from the unbalanced and lopsided adulation of the "beast." But worship of a power principle was never the teaching of the rabbi Jesus, the "faithful witness" who preached the healing of human relationships and the love of one's neighbor within the context of God's revelation in Judaism, the Jesus who modeled sacred partnership with the woman called "the Magdalene."

Now that we understand the meaning of the number 666 and the real nature of the warning that the prophet-author of the Apocalypse was trying to convey, perhaps it is not too late to prevent the final conflagration on planet Earth. The Apocalypse warns of the holocaust inherent in the worship of raw power. All nations of Earth seem to be involved in the adulation of a sun god, "seated at the right hand"—champion of a left-brain value system!—who comes in power and vindication, scorching the earth with his wrath, meting out destruction and punishment on the wicked, and leaving only devastation in his wake.

It seems clear that the author of Apocalypse wished to expose the dire legacy of the high Christology of the Church emerging at the end of the first century. The evolving Church, influenced by Greek and Roman mythologies and by the imminent Second Coming envisioned by Paul, had revised the earlier understanding of a very human Jesus preached by the original apostles who had walked with him during his ministry in Israel. Although hints of that earlier understanding remain with us, embedded by gematria in the canonical Gospels, a dramatic new understanding was being developed styling Jesus the Christ as the *Kyrios* or "bearer" of the Spirit of the New Age of Pisces—the Lord of "the Fishes."

8

THE TURNING
OF THE AGE

Since the very dawn of human experience, people have scanned the night skies in awe, watching the movements of the moon and stars and marveling at their orderly procession across the heavens. In the century preceding the birth of Jesus, interest in astronomy and astrology was strong, and those who searched the heavens for their signs were expectant because they were aware of the rising sign in the precession of the equinoxes—the sign of Pisces, the Fishes. The priests and astrologers of the time watched and waited, savoring the prophecies of the coming age, longing for the revelation of its avatar. When they heard the story, told and retold, of the charismatic rabbi Yeshua crucified by Rome's decree and raised from the dead, they recognized the mythic energies they had been expecting. The itinerant Jewish teacher was eventually appropriated by the Hellenized culture of the Roman Empire as the incarnation of the Spirit of the Age. He became Kyrios, the "bearer" and Lord of Pisces.[1] The Greek phrase *Ιησους Χριστος Θεου Υιος Σοτερ* (Jesus Christ, Son of God Savior) was used to form the acronym ICHTHYS, which means "fish," and soon the followers of Jesus used the symbol of a fish to identify themselves with the new cult. The oral tradition surrounding Jesus was marked with frequent allusions to fish and fishermen. The stories told by his disciples included his miraculous multiplication of loaves and fishes, the call to Peter the fisherman, the spectacular catch, and the 153 fishes in the net. The kingdom of God, says the Gospel, is like a dragnet thrown into the sea that catches fish of every kind (Matt. 13:47). Subsequent generations universally associated Christianity with the fish. Even the traditional practice of eating fish on Fridays has its roots in the faith of the fishes.

In the idiom of the first century, the precessional age of Aries the Ram was succeeded by that of Jesus, whose epithet among Christians was "the Fish." This explains why the popular cult of the solar deity Mithras was replaced by that of Jesus. Mithraism was a religion that had originated in Persia and was practiced enthusiastically in the Roman legions; it was related to the precession of the equinoxes, through the signs of the zodiac, and celebrated the slaying of the bull (symbol of the Age of Taurus) by the hero of the "new age"—Aries. The cult had many similarities with Christianity, including the December 25 birth date of the savior-hero, Mithras. In the logic of the precession, in which the zodiacal signs move backward, the Age of Aries gave way to the Age of Pisces with its newly articulated myth of Christ, the hero-avatar of the "Fishes."

According to the Gospel of Matthew, Magi (astrologers) from the East had noticed the unusual "star of Bethlehem" in the sky at the time of the birth of Jesus. Some astronomers have identified this celestial configuration as the conjunction of Jupiter and Saturn in the sign of Pisces, which occurred from May to December in 7 B.C., an event probably perceived by many to herald the Age of Pisces and announce the birth of the long-awaited Messiah of the Jewish people. [2]

THE LAMB AND THE FISHES

The passing of the Age of Aries, the Ram, seems to echo in frequent New Testament references to Jesus as the Lamb of God, with its connotations of sacrifice on behalf of the people. His crucifixion was viewed as the culmination of the dying age, the death of the Ram, and his resurrection as "Christ" or "Anointed One" coincided with the rising sign of the Fishes.

In the Fourth Gospel John the Baptist greets his cousin Jesus at their meeting on the banks of the Jordan River with the pronouncement: "Behold the Lamb of God" (John 2:29). The image of the lamb is used very dramatically by the author of the Book of Revelation, who repeatedly refers to Jesus as the "butchered Lamb." After the death of Jesus, the "Lamb of God," pious Jews continued to make their offerings of lambs and turtledoves for only four more decades before the final destruction of their Temple and the suspension of the associated cult of animal sacrifice practiced there. With the total destruction of the Temple of Jerusalem on the ninth of Av, A.D. 70, the practice of offering animal holocausts as demanded by Jewish law was officially terminated. In occult terminology, the Age of Aries was officially over; the Age of Pisces had already begun.

It might be said that during the course of several centuries following his crucifixion, the Jewish charismatic king Jesus was deliberately adopted throughout the Roman Empire as the bridge between the dying and rising astrological ages, since he was characterized by his followers as embodying the archetypes of both the Lamb and the Fish. The study of the gematria of the New Testament writings, particularly the Fourth Gospel, assures us that the initiates of the wisdom schools recognized Jesus as Lord of the Fishes, represented by the number 888—that is, 111 × 8— "the new day," the epitome of "regeneration." In the historical person Jesus of Nazareth they discovered that the archetypal myth of the dying and rising god—the sacrificed bridegroom/king of the hieros gamos mythology—had become flesh. The birth of the Savior Son of God—the Sun of the New Age—was reflected in the number 888—the gematria of the name Jesus (*Iησους*) at which, according to Paul, "every knee should bend" (Phil. 2:10). This faith is coded into several passages in the Gospels. For example, Matthew 1:23 reads: "Behold a virgin shall conceive and bear a son and he shall be called Emmanuel, that is interpreted, God with us." The gematria of this entire verse is 8880.

It now seems clear that a group of philosophers in the first century of the current era established a system of doctrines to give continuity to the underlying values of their civilization. The cross-pollination of cultures created unprecedented turmoil during the period of the Roman Empire. The Roman emperors who claimed divinity for themselves and insisted on being worshiped were universally hated by repressed peoples in the outlying provinces of the empire. Apocalyptic writings of the period attest to the sufferings of conquered provinces, and the people of Palestine yearned to see the saving power of their God, the prophesied "day of the Lord." The phrase "the salvation of our God" occurs in Isaiah 52:10; its Hebrew gematria is 888, and in Hebrew, the name *Yeshua* (Jesus) means "Yahweh saves." Paul and other contemporary Christians expected the world to come soon to a violent end and believed that in the "age to come" Jesus would miraculously appear in glory to usher in the "kingdom of God."

Fear, spawned by cataclysmic events that are recorded during the first century—droughts and famines, volcanic eruptions and earthquakes—was widespread in the Roman Empire during the first century of the current era. Many expected to see the world's abrupt end, and these deep-seated fears are reflected in the Gospels, culminating in the prophetic words of Jesus that the stones of the Temple would not be left one on top of the other (Mark 13:2). "But woe to those who are with child or have infants the breast in those days!" (Mark 13:17). On the ninth of Av, A.D. 70, Roman soldiers forced the men of Jerusalem to climb to the top of the Temple walls and cast the buildings' stones into the streets below. The residents of Jerusalem were aghast! The date was the anniversary of the destruction of their beloved Temple by the victorious armies of the Babylonian king Nebuchadnezzar in 586 B.C.

The infant Christian community in Jerusalem did not survive the destruction of the Temple and the Holy City. The Good News of Jesus had been carried to outlying cities in the empire where it germinated and later flourished in Christian communities far from the city of its origin. In later centuries the Church of Rome was characterized by its adherents as the "New Jerusalem," and the teachers of Christianity named themselves the spiritual heirs of Israel, thereby appropriating the promises of Yahweh to his chosen people celebrated in the psalms and prophecies of the Hebrew Scriptures.

In his wisdom Jesus had recommended that new wineskins be found to contain the new cultural thrust of his "Way" and the "Good News" of God's immanent reign—the ideals he envisioned for the dawning of the "age to come"—the astrological Age of Pisces. Who abbreviated the initials of the honorific phrase "Jesus Christ, Son of God, Savior" to form the word *ichthys*? Who traced the first fish symbol in the sand to identify himself as a follower of the Jewish Messiah? Mark's Gospel, the first written, mentions the feeding of the multitudes with the five barley loaves and two fishes, and each of the later Gospels records a similar event. The apostles are styled as fishermen from the very earliest sources of Christian tradition. Tertullian (A.D. 155–200) and Clement of Alexandria (150–215) both used the fish as a symbol for Jesus, and Augustine followed the practice as well.[3] Christian homilists referred to their parishioners as *pisciculi*, the "little fishes," and dubbed the baptismal font the *piscina*, the "fish pond." In the final chapter of John's Gospel, the catch of 153 large fishes represents the entire church of the "Fishes," and in Luke 5:6 "the multitude of fishes" (ιχθυων πολυ) is 153×4^2. When we remember that four is the basic number for "flesh and blood" and matter/earth, this phrase about the spectacular catch of fishes proves to be a metaphor for Christian converts, reinforced by the declaration "I am the Way" (John 14:6) which yields the sum 1224, the gematria also of ιχθγες—"fishes"!

Because the fish/fisherman theme permeates early Christianity, it seems extraordinary that Jesus in the Gospels never once refers to himself as a fish or even a fisherman but rather as "shepherd," as "bridegroom," and as heir to the "vine-yard of Israel." It is the testimony of the later community of believers that his apostles became "fishers of men." By the time the Gospels were written, the image of the fish and the identifi-cation of Jesus as the Lord of the Piscean Age were already well entrenched in Christian consciousness.

The New Testament phrases that tie in to the sacred numbers of the ancient cosmological canon (666, 888, 1080, 1224, 1746, 3168) seem to have been deliberately coined to adapt the Jewish messianic martyr Jesus to the framework of existing religious beliefs in the Mediterranean region. In the mystery religions of the Hellenistic world, mystical regeneration by means of sacra-mental participation in the death and sacrifice of a redeemer god was practiced in the cults of the Egyptian god Osiris, Babylonian Tammuz, and Greek Adonis and Dionysus. Significant elements of early Christian doctrine and liturgy, particularly the cultic "thanksgiving" eucharistic meal and baptismal rites, can be inter-preted as an attempt to adapt the rising cult of the historical Jesus, "Son of God," into the mystery cults of the region, particu-larly those of the gods Mithras and Dionysus. In examining the stories in the Gospels concerning the multiplication of the loaves and fishes, it is significant that references repeated in all four Gospels are made to *two fishes*—the astrological sign of the dawn-ing Age. At the Eucharistic meals of the early Christians, fish was usually consumed in addition to bread and wine. Establishing Jesus as Kyrios took several centuries, but eventually Jesus was enthroned as universal Lord of the Age—symbolically seated on a celestial throne at God's right hand as described in the Book of Revelation.

The new religion called Christianity was an amalgam or marriage of the Jewish faith in the one true God of all creation with the philosophy of the classical world of the Greeks. The measurements of the New Jerusalem confirm this theory of synthesis and syncretism: a combining of the sacred tenets of the covenant of Moses and the Jewish wisdom tradition with the astrological signs of the zodiac, the wisdom of the classical philosophers, and the cosmology of the whole Greco-Roman world.[4]

The Historical Jesus

The Gospels suggest that Jesus did not come to establish a new religion, but rather to fulfill the prophecies of the Jewish nation and to preach a new understanding of God's continuous presence with the *anawim*—the poor, the oppressed, and the disenfranchised—as articulated in the tradition of the Hebrew prophets. The radical message of "Emmanuel"—"God with us!"—was demonstrated when Jesus overturned the money changers' tables in the Temple, to the outrage and chagrin of the elite group of corrupt priests presiding over the cult worship and animal sacrifices of the Temple—"the shepherds who pasture themselves instead of the sheep" castigated in Ezekiel 34 and Jeremiah 23.

Jesus is portrayed in the Gospels as a charismatic Jewish teacher, healer, and prophet. He was a son of his people and the heir to God's vineyard, Israel. He is often an antiestablishment hero. He is compassionate toward the poor and the disenfranchised and a champion of justice on their behalf. The original militant portrayal of Jesus may have been mitigated by later censors of the early pericopes and stories circulated in the oral tradition surrounding his ministry. This censorship appeared necessary to avoid offending citizens of the Roman Empire or alienating potential Gentile converts to Christianity.[5] The Gospels, written after the Jewish rebellion of A.D. 67–73, were given a "pro-Roman" and "anti-Jewish" character that reflected a later attitude of reconciliation with Rome, but may not have been the original message or attitude of Jesus. In his recent volume *The Sword of Constantine,* James Carroll characterizes the Gospel allegation that the Jews executed Jesus as a tragic historical error whose dire long-range consequences have proven to be incalculable.

The Jesus portrayed by Christian doctrine of later centuries is celestial Victor, Ruler, and Judge. He is the Son of God and Lord of the Universe, the second person of the Most Holy Trinity, the Only Begotten Son, and according to the Nicene Creed, "of one being with the Father." He ascended into heaven and is the object of Christian worship on Sunday. This is high Christology: the Jesus Christ of Christian tradition is a male solar divinity par excellence, portrayed in the image of the sun gods of Egypt (Ra), Greece (Apollo), Rome (Mithras and Sol Invictus), and Persia (Ahura Mazda).

But we are also well acquainted with another Jesus—the Jesus of the Gospels. This other Jesus, the "historical" Jesus, was a charismatic Jewish teacher who walked the dusty roads between Judea's villages, healed the sick, and preached a dynamic message of reconciliation, relationship, and social justice. This Jesus was an incarnation of God's compassion, some even said of the "Sophia"—Holy Wisdom—for it was her dove that alighted on his shoulder at his baptism. He was anointed by the woman with the alabaster jar at the banquet in Bethany. And he was sentenced to an ignominious torture and death by the Roman procurator, crucified as an insurrectionist under the supervision of a Roman centurion. And for his garment, "they cast lots," in fulfillment of the prophecy of Psalm 22. This Jesus—the Jewish Yeshua—fled whenever the people tried to proclaim him king and died on the cross at Golgotha, a radical illustration of the "woundedness" of a God—the vulnerability of a deity who allows free will—whose prophets are universally reviled, scorned, and tortured.

Beyond the orthodox interpretation of the Gospel story there is another story, a secret version of the life of Jesus branded heretical and forced underground. Although some communities came to believe in a high "solar" Christology of Jesus, the celestial and omnipotent king and "Cloud-Rider" (as noted above, an ancient epithet of the Canaanite sun god Ba'al), there were also communities who loved Jesus as a brother, friend, and guide. The low Christology of the first-century Ebionite Christians and later Arian heretics of the fourth to sixth centuries in Western Europe shows a strong continuity with the original Jerusalem Christians under the leadership of James, the brother of Jesus.[6] Adherents to these heresies insisted on the true and full humanity of Jesus and his "sonship" as that of a chosen "vessel" committed to God's purposes, "a faithful servant" and dutiful son obedient to the will of his father even to the death.

The teachings of later Church fathers and exegetes successfully transformed the Jewish rabbi/messiah into an oriental potentate, gradually developing the high Christology articulated in the Nicene Creed (A.D. 325) that equated Jesus with God: "Light from light, true God from true God, begotten, not made, of one being with the Father." On her way to this doctrinal proclamation, the "orthodox" Church branded the Ebionites heretical and subsequently hounded the Arian Christians of Western Europe out of existence. These early sects believed in the fully human nature of Jesus, a man chosen by God to reveal a new relationship between the eternal Holy One and his human children. This revelation was articulated in the teachings of Jesus and modeled in the community who followed him, epitomized in the person of his most devoted and beloved follower, the Mary called "the Magdalene" by all generations of Christians.

9

THE HOLY NAME
OF MARY

The Divine Office, the liturgy of the hours published by authority of Pope Paul VI, contains a brief note for the feast day of Mary Magdalene on July 22 that says that devotion to Saint Mary Magdalene was widespread in the Western Church by the twelfth century. While this may be true, it is a bit misleading, suggesting that devotion to Mary Magdalene grew to a gradual crescendo. In fact, devotion to Mary Magdalene in the twelfth century was only a shadow of the honor in which she was held by the earliest Christians and by certain Gnostic communities before the fifth century. The symbolic numbers associated with Mary Magdalene indicate that she was "First Lady" in the foundation myth of Christianity. When the memory of her preeminence in early Christianity surfaced in the twelfth century, it was nearly wiped out by the Albigensian Crusade ruthlessly suppressing the "Church of Amor" and other heresies dangerous to the hegemony of the Roman Catholic Church.

As we have noted in the preceding chapters, sacred numbers revealed in New Testament gematria demonstrate that certain phrases and epithets of the Christian Scriptures contain hidden meanings coded in their sums. Once again, I urge my readers to turn to the cited works of John Michell and David Fideler for detailed scholarly research on this fascinating subject and to consult the research of Del Washburn in *Theomatics* for the clusters surrounding significant numbers. In 1993 I had an opportunity to meet John Michell and to ask him if he had ever calculated the numbers attached to Mary Magdalene to see if they might hold significance about her role in the early Christian community. He admitted that he had not calculated her gematria and strongly suggested that I take on the task. What I discovered in the numbers associated with the woman called "the Magdalene" was more than significant; it was earth-shaking! Hidden in the powerful gematria of the epithet η Μαγδαληνη is the lost "goddess" of Christian mythology, the beloved counterpart of the sacrificed bridegroom. She is the other "fish" of the zodiac symbol for Pisces. How could this vital information have been denied for two millennia? Its importance is monumental; the consequences of its loss, staggering!

THE MARIAM OF THE GOSPELS

The name of Mary is borne by several different women in the Gospels. The mother of Jesus is Mary, as is the sister of Lazarus—as well as the woman called "the Magdalene" by the early Christians. Another Mary mentioned several times is the "mother of James" but since the name of the brother of Jesus most often mentioned in the Scriptures is James, this could be a reference to the mother of both men—Jesus and James. As already mentioned, the popular female name comes from the root word meaning "ocean" or "salt sea," acknowledged as the womb of all life on this planet. In the canonical Gospels, the name Mary is spelled in two different ways: "Maria" and "Mariam." When I first examined the Greek texts of the Gospels to study this problem, I thought perhaps the spelling was a mistake. Maybe careless copyists had accidentally deleted the final "m" from the Hebrew name Miryam shared by these several women. But the practice of gematria indicates that each of the two variant spellings is highly significant and for this reason, it seems very likely that both spellings of the name were used specifically to express the prominence of the women named Mary in the New Testament community.

The sum of the letters in Mariam is 192. This number represents the epitome of four—actually 3×4^3. That is significant, for as we have seen, four is the number of Earth, as is reflected in such phrases as "the four corners of the earth" and "the four winds," and 444 was identified with "flesh and blood"—all the living creatures of the earth, but especially human beings. As we have seen, common expressions like "the four elements," the "four seasons," and "four directions" also reflect this concept of four related to physical matter and "mother" earth. In several languages the name of Mary is associated with *mother, matter,* and *material,* all of which are related to the Sanskrit *matr* (Latin: *mater, matron*; Greek: *matrix*). In Latin, *maritare* is "to wed," a word whose derivations appear in Romance languages and in the English "marry."

The shape Plato associates with the element earth is the cube, and even (as opposed to odd) integers were considered feminine in the ancient world. Three times the cube of four, that is, 3×4^3 or $3(4 \times 4 \times 4)$, equals 192, the gematria of "Mariam." Because of the associations of the number four with the feminine, "matter," and "flesh and blood," the gematria of Mariam reflects the concept of "mother," and thus all the Mariams in the Gospel story share in this meaning. The name "Mariam" when it appears in the Greek texts of the Gospels with the final letter *m* thus bears universal connotations of the feminine "container"—the flesh-and-blood vessel or womb of the Mother—through the computation of its gematria.

But in the case of Mary Magdalene, the gematria of the epithet "the Magdalene" must also be added to her name. In the instances when her name would be *Mariam*, the addition of the epithet "the Magdalene," η Μαγδαληνη—meaning "the elevated," "great," or "tower"—leads to a gematria of 345. Because of the *colel* of +1 (and in this case +2) that can be added to or subtracted from any number without altering its symbolic significance, the name of this special intimate of Jesus is very closely associated with the "eternal feminine"—the virgin or wisdom goddess whose symbolic number is seven—for 343 is 7^3, the epitome of seven. This number also links the Magdalene with the Greek goddess Pallas Athene, who was also associated with seven by the gematria of her name: for Pallas (Παλλας) equals 342 by gematria, and the gematria for Athene (AΘηνη) is 76 (plus the *colel* +1 = 77). The distinctive gematria 345 may be one reason Gnostic Christians, who were accused of using "numbers theology," associated Mary Magdalene with the Sophia—Holy Wisdom—in so many of their sacred texts. This important connection has been obscured for 1,500 years and has only recently come to light with the translation of the Gnostic codices hidden in jars in about A.D. 400 and discovered in 1945 in the Egyptian desert near Nag Hammadi.

THE GODDESS NUMBER SEVEN

We have noted that seven is one of the significant numbers in the symbolic system of the ancient world that relate to the "sacred feminine," and we are familiar with its standing for the completion of a cycle of time. We have noted its virginal aspect and have examined the fact that seven divides the lunar month of twenty-eight days into four weeks corresponding to the four phases of the moon, also intimately related to the feminine. Since a woman's menstrual cycle is governed by the moon, the association between the moon and women was made very early in prehistory. The relief carving of the Goddess figure from the Neolithic period discovered at Laussel holds a curved horn displaying thirteen cuts that represent the thirteen lunar months of the female fertility cycle and the words *month* and *menses* derive from this association with the moon (Greek μηνη). Seven days constitute a week: "and God blessed the seventh day and sanctified it." A menorah has seven candles, and "clean" animals were brought into the ark by sevens (Gen. 7:2). Jacob served seven years for each of his brides, Leah and Rachel, and in ancient Israel a field lay fallow for a "sabbatical year" after six years of cultivation. Pharaoh dreamed of seven fat cows and seven lean, each set representing a period of years according to Joseph's famous interpretation (Gen. 42:25).

In Christian doctrine, as previously noted, there are seven deadly sins, seven cardinal virtues, seven gifts of the Holy Spirit, and seven fruits of the spiritual life. Jesus tells his apostle Peter to forgive not seven times, but seventy times seven times, meaning infinitely! Seven designates eternal, ethical, spiritual, and celestial rather than created things and bears strong associations with the sacred feminine principle, intuition, and wisdom.

Because of the obvious difficulty of getting letters and numbers to correspond exactly, the close connection of the cube of seven (343) to the names of Mariam the Magdalene (345) and Pallas Athene (342) is illuminating. The number seven was associated with the Holy Spirit and with Holy Wisdom—the Sophia sought by philosophers (literally, "lovers of wisdom") who, according to a first-century work called *The Wisdom of Solomon*, was described as "the immaculate mirror of God's energy" and "spouse of God."[1] These correspondences of the goddess number with Mary the Magdalene are crucial to the correct understanding of the Gospel story. In long-standing tradition, it was she, understood by early Gnostics as an incarnation of the Sophia, who anointed Jesus at the banquet at Bethany—ritually proclaiming him *messiah*, which literally means "the anointed one." By using an epithet for this Mary that equated her by gematria with Sophia, and "Holy Wisdom," the architects of the New Covenant were naming this woman the "sister-bride" of their Lord, just as surely as wisdom was the bride sought by the youthful King Solomon according to the wisdom literature of Judaism.

Virgo—"Our Lady"

In *The Lost Language of Symbolism,* Harold Bayley shows the primitive roots of Indo-European words. *Mag,* root of Mary Magdalene's epithet, combines the root syllable *ma* (the feminine) with *ag/ak* (great) and means "great woman." We find this syllable in English words like *magnificent,* and *magnanimous* which retain the feminine flavor (elegant, generous). Why did the authors of the Christian Gospels desire that the name of the "great Mary" in the Gospels be identified with the Goddess of the ancient world? To answer this, we must consult the signs of the zodiac. We know that first-century initiates and intellectuals of the Roman Empire were intensely interested in the precession of the equinoxes and were aware that their civilization was poised at the threshold of the age of the rising constellation Pisces. The sign opposite to Pisces on the zodiac wheel is Virgo, the axis forming a partnership of two astrological signs. The author of the Apocalypse of John associated Virgo with Demeter,[2] the grain goddess of the Greek pantheon, and by extension probably also with Ishtar of the Babylonians. This goddess was Queen of Earth and harvests; among her many gifts, fertility was the greatest. Literal or physical virginity was emphatically not an attribute of the Great Goddess. She represented Earth as mother and was "whole unto herself"—the "creative matrix." Her astrological symbol ♍, is the unique combination of the Latin letters *M* and *V* that represent the sacred feminine as supernal mother/container, the sacred chalice or "grail"—Our Lady.

John Michell and other scholars of esoteric traditions suggest that early converts to the "Good News" constructed Christian doctrine to correspond to traditional tenets of their culture and milieu, while pouring them into the "new wineskins" mentioned in the Gospels—deliberately creating a new foundation myth and new doctrines to carry them. The gematria in the Gospels seems to confirm this point, not once but over and over. The church fathers in the second and third centuries anathematized this use of numerical analysis for interpretation of Scripture, thereby obscuring many of its truths for nearly two millennia. I believe that one of the fundamental tenets of the "Good News" proclaimed in Christianity—"the stone the builders rejected"—was the mandala of sacred partnership—the ✡.

On seven of the eight lists that name several women who were followers and companions of Jesus, Mary Magdalene is mentioned first; only once—in John 19:25 at the foot of the cross—is the mother of Jesus mentioned before the Magdalene. From the very earliest Gospels of Mark and Matthew it is apparent that the Mary who was understood to be preeminent was not the mother of Jesus but the Mary called the Magdalene. In fact, this is indicated in the Gospel that states that the women who went to the tomb were Mary the Magdalene and "the other Mary" (Matt. 28:1). Of these two women, which was most likely "first lady" in the community?

In Judaism, the married state was the established norm. It was the solemn obligation of every Jewish father to find a suitable wife for his son before the young man's twentieth birthday. A man without a wife was not to be trusted, according to the wisdom tradition of first-century Judaism: "A man with no wife becomes a homeless wanderer. Who will trust . . . a man who has no nest but lodges where night overtakes him?" (Eccles. 36:25). Ecclesiastes, written in Hebrew between 200 and 175 B.C. by an author devoted to the law, the prophets, and the wisdom of Israel, was widely taught at the time of Jesus. While the Gospel tradition characterizes Jesus as an itinerant preacher, it is obvious in the Gospels that his home base is Bethany. When Jesus was teaching in the vicinity of Jerusalem, it appears that he resided in Bethany. One interpretation of the raising of Lazarus in John 11 suggests that Mary, the sister of Lazarus, was performing official mourning for her brother—"sitting *shiva*"—and was not permitted to leave her post unless her husband requested her presence.

Unless one is familiar with the mourning practices of a Jewish family, one would not discern anything unusual from the situation narrated in John 11:28: "she [Martha] went away and quietly called Mary her sister, saying, 'The Master is here and calls thee.' As soon as she [Mary] heard this, she rose quickly and came to him." For someone aware of the Jewish traditions of *shiva*, this passage inadvertently supports the view that Mary of Bethany was the wife of Jesus, who awaited his summons before leaving her mourning to approach him.[3]

According to the legend of the Sangraal,[4] by the time the Gospel stories were committed to papyrus, the immediate family of Jesus had fled into exile in France and their close connection to him had been deliberately obscured for their own protection. But the epithet "the Magdalene" was retained in the stories told about the intimate friend of Jesus who had accompanied him during his ministry. As stated earlier, the name of Mariam the Magdalene contained a coded gematria identifying its bearer with the number seven, the number associated with various goddesses, and hence, the sacred feminine. In their system of symbol and number, it was this Mary who was the beloved companion and counterpart of the Lord of the Fishes. In the Gospel of Philip found among the Gnostic texts at Nag Hammadi, she is the companion and *koinonōs* of Jesus—his "consort" whom he loved more than the disciples and whom he kissed often on the mouth.[5] Philip goes on to explain that the apostles were jealous of this intimacy between the Savior and his beloved.

The actual Greek letters for the epithet "the Magdalene," η Μαγδαληνη, are very distinctive. The *-ene (hnh)* ending is not a correct or typical one for designating a person from a particular town or region; to denote a person from a particular region or town, the ending should be *-ios.* If Mary were from a town called "Magdala," the correct Greek spelling of her epithet would be Μαγδαλαιος, "Magdalaios." There must be a different reason this unique epithet was coined specifically for this Mary. My research affirms that it had nothing whatever to do with her hometown, although this is a widely believed hypothesis. According to contemporary records, the small fishing village on the shores of Lake Kinneret that is now called Magdala was known by the Greek name Taricheae during the time of Jesus. According to Jewish historians, the ruins of this ancient site were renamed Magdala by later Christians who (mistakenly, in my opinion) believed that Mary Magdalene had come from that general region, called Magada or Dalmanutha. These Christians were clearly searching for a logical reason for the epithet that clung to her and lit on the place of origin as a likely possibility—most probably because of the perceived similarity of the first syllable in the words "Magada" and "Magdalene," but possibly also because an ancient fishing village on the same site was called by an Aramaic name, Migdal Nunayah, the "Tower of the Fishermen."

I believe this assumption—that Mary Magdalene was from "Magdala"—to be a colossal error that, whether by accident or by design, obscures the true origin of her epithet: the "tower/stronghold." The Hebrew word *magdala (migdol)* means "tower-stronghold" or "elevated." I believe the epithet specifically associates her with the "tower-stronghold of Daughter of Zion" sent into exile whence it is prophesied she shall eventually be rescued:

As for you, O Magdal-eder, watchtower of the flock,
O stronghold of the Daughter of Zion
The former dominion will be restored to you;
Kingship will come to the Daughter of Jerusalem.
Why do you now cry aloud?
Have you no king? . . .
For now you must leave the city,
And camp in the open field,
And from there you shall be rescued.

MICAH 4:8–10

Just as the early Christians found prophecies in the words of Isaiah and Hosea that threw light on their experience of their Lord, Jesus, I believe they discovered that this passage from Micah illuminated the historical role of Mary Magdalene, their Lady. It is this Mary who is, metaphorically, the "Tower of the Flock" and symbolically representative of her people— Israel/Zion. This theme is reinforced in references to the "Widow Zion" in the Hebrew Book of Lamentations, whose lament for her bridegroom is liturgically celebrated on the ninth of Av in commemoration of the destruction of the Temple on two separate occasions, in 586 B.C. and A.D. 70. It also mirrors the Christian characterization of Mary Magdalene as the model for the Church, for contemplative orders of religious, and her story is a metaphor for the journey of each soul longing for union with her bridegroom/beloved. It is inevitably she who cries over the feet of her bridegroom in religious art depicting the removal of Jesus from the cross. And it is also she who, in Christian art, always carries the alabaster jar of precious nard, the fragrance of the bride in the Song of Solomon. This in itself should tell us something, since that beautiful and erotic poem is a redaction of poetry from the cult of the sacrificed bridegroom indigenous to the Near East.[6]

There is a significant Greek parallel for the distinctive -ene ending of Magdalene that makes sense. The ending on the name of the Greek goddess Athene (Aθηνη) is the same three letters, and apparently both names—the Magdalene and Athene—were consciously coined with their distinctive spellings for the same reason: the combination of letters provided the gematria necessary to carry the intended archetype "Wisdom" associated with the symbolic value of their sacred numbers.

THE FAMILY OF JESUS

Christians for centuries have puzzled over several Gospel passages in which Jesus seems to be estranged from his mother and siblings. These passages seem to be attempts on the part of the Gospel writers to downplay the family connection—the kin and bloodline of Jesus. Possibly, it was felt to be necessary to obscure these connections in order to protect the legitimate heirs of the royal lineage from physical danger. Or, even more likely, it was done to emphasize the legitimacy of powerful well-known Christian leaders like Paul and Timothy who were not related to Jesus but were bearers of the dynamic new religion being promulgated throughout the Roman Empire in his name.

Several pagan gods were said to have been born of virgin mothers, but there is no other hint in the earliest Gospel that Mary, the *mother* of Jesus, is understood to be the goddess-partner of the anointed Messiah, although that is ultimately the paradigm, borrowed from Egyptian and Greek mythology, that the Christian Church later concretized in its Hellenistic mother-and-son dogma. By the simple fact of the anointing of Jesus the exalted role of bride and partner is identified with "the woman with the alabaster jar." And the woman named in John's Gospel as the one who anointed Jesus was Mary, the sister of Lazarus. Her anointing of the Messiah was the exclusive prerogative of the priestess/bride in the ancient rite of the sacred marriage indigenous to the Near East, since the anointing prefigured the consummation of the nuptials during the marital act when the feminine secretions "anoint" the masculine.

In John's Gospel it is clearly stated in two separate places (John 11:2 and 12:3) that the woman who anointed Jesus and "wiped his feet dry with her hair" was the sister of Lazarus. I believe that it is she whom the community also later identified with the epithet the Magdalene, since in the ancient cults celebrating the sacred marriage it is always the bride who anoints her bridegroom in the actual nuptial rite—foreshadowing events consummated in the privacy of the bridal chamber. In these same religious rites of the ancient Near East, it is the bride who, accompanied by her women, returns to the tomb (usually on the third day) and encounters her beloved resurrected in the garden. The motif of the resurrection of a god after three days and nights in the netherworld goes back to the Sumerian prototype, as do the epithets of "bridegroom," "shepherd," and "anointed."[7]

After his resurrection, when the wife of Jesus was spirited away from the dangerous political turmoil in Jerusalem, the entire community of followers of Jesus was in total disarray. By the time the apostles and friends of Jesus realized the importance of the story of their beloved rabbi and organized themselves to attempt to preach and heal in his name, his wife and her closest associates had already disappeared into the mists of obscurity, probably finding political exile in Alexandria. The infant church in Jerusalem went on without Mary, but stories (pericopes) about her anointing of Jesus and her Easter encounter with him at the empty tomb in the garden continued to be circulated. There was a woman, the stories insist, who once anointed Jesus, a woman named Mary who was closely—even intimately—associated with him, a woman who kissed his feet and dried them with her hair, a woman whose unique epithet was known and whispered—"the Magdalene." It was explicitly this distinctive epithet that identified her to the community as the sister-bride—the true partner and counterpart of Jesus—in spite of the fact that the memory of their marriage relationship was obscured.

The later convert Paul never mentions Mary Magdalene in his letters (A.D. 53–67), written before the Gospels (A.D. 70–95), nor does Luke mention her in the Book of Acts of the Apostles (A.D. 63–65), yet Mary Magdalene plays an extremely important role in each of the four canonical Gospels where she is the first to discover the empty tomb on Easter morning. And the story of the anointing is "told and retold in memory of her" (Mark 14:9) just as Jesus intended it should be. The question is, why?

If Paul is the first to write about the Christian Way, why does he ignore the stories of Mary of Bethany and "the Magdalene" that the Gospel authors include? One feasible answer is the fact that

Paul doesn't say much at all about the actual human Jesus or his ministry on Earth. He is more concerned with the risen Christ than with the historical figure of Jesus. But I consider it also likely that the close friends and blood relations of Jesus did not fully trust disclosing her true identity to Paul, who had no personal acquaintance with Jesus or Mary and who, after all, had persecuted members of the Jerusalem community before his startling conversion on the road to Damascus.

The stories of Magdalene circulated in the oral tradition, but they were not committed to writing until after Paul was dead. Was it too dangerous to speak aloud about this woman in the first generation of Christianity? Perhaps the memory of the persecutions instigated by Paul before his conversion was still fresh and painful. Luke, who was allegedly a close associate of Paul, is the only Gospel author who displaces the pericope of the anointing of Jesus at Bethany and calls the woman a sinner, an assertion that John's Gospel tries in two places to correct by naming the woman who anointed Jesus—Mary of Bethany, the sister of Lazarus (John 11:2 and 12:3). Did Luke not know the identity of the bride? Or did he deliberately dissociate her from her prominent role inaugurating the passion narrative in order to protect her identity? Does fear for her personal safety explain why Magdalene's story is so deeply shrouded in mythology—the "greatest story never told"? I believe that it does.

The similarities between the Gospel sequence of the anointing, death, and resurrection of the bridegroom of Israel and the more ancient liturgies from the fertility cults of other gods and heroes Dumuzi, Ba'al, and Tammuz are nothing short of remarkable. Why is this obvious connection ignored by Christian exegetes and Bible scholars? Are these ancient roots of Christianity too pagan for their taste? Is the inclusion of the bride/beloved still unpalatable, even after two millennia of repression? Is it not yet time to resurrect the hieros gamos of the eternal bride and bridegroom that images God as intimate partners—the joyful partnership that could at last restore the mythology of "sacred union" at the heart of the original Christian community?

It is probable that the first-century citizens of the Roman Empire recognized in the three Marias of the Gospels echoes of the great "triple goddess" of the ancient world in her three distinct aspects—maiden, mother, and crone. As the years unfolded, and the obscured flesh and blood (444) wife of Jesus did not return, the Christian patriarchs of the Hellenized Roman Empire, including John Chrysostom, the fourth-century Patriarch of Constantinople, ventured to identify in her place the *mother* of Jesus. They even insisted on the literal virginity (*parthenos* in Greek) of Mary, probably to break the perceived incestuous and licentious relationships in the myths of some of the gods and goddesses of the Greek and Roman pantheons. The "Blessed Virgin" became the Virgo pole of the axis of the New Age of Pisces. But the gematria of her name indicates that in the original New Testament pericopes it was not the mother of Jesus, but rather the Mary called "the Magdalene" who was originally identified as first lady. As the sister-bride archetype suggests, Mary Magdalene bears associations with both earth and wisdom goddesses of the pagan pantheons, of whom Inanna, "Queen of Heaven," was the ancient Sumerian prototype. These associations were later transferred to the Virgin Mother of Jesus, while the Magdalene was given the now familiar epithets "prostitute" and "pentitent."

THE 153 FISHES AND THE NEW JERUSALEM

I am greatly indebted to John Michell for his elucidation of the measurements of the New Jerusalem in Revelation and the sacred numbers of the Holy City that is the "bride" of Jesus, "the Lamb." In *The Dimensions of Paradise* Michell discusses at length the esoteric geometry of the last chapter of John's Gospel.[8] A further and very significant explanation of this New Testament passage is given by David Fideler in *Jesus Christ, Sun of God*.[9] I hope many readers will turn to the works of these scholars for more detailed explanations of the sacred numbers and geometry of this and other New Testament texts.

In the story found in John 21, the risen Jesus, we remember, was standing at dawn on the shore of the Sea of Tiberius and seven of his disciples were out in a boat, fishing with no success. From the shore where he is cooking fish, Jesus instructs them to cast their nets on the starboard side, and as we read on, it seems slightly odd that there should be a catch of exactly 153 fishes in their net. Who in that early dawn was counting the fish they caught? Who even cared? And why would there be 153 fishes and not some other number? Since by now we realize that nothing is without meaning, and that numbers in Scripture often have symbolic importance, we must pause to examine the story of the fishermen and the fishes in the unbroken net, hoping to discover the hidden meaning of the passage. The interpretation of this intricate "geometry story problem" offered by John Michell and David Fideler helps us fully appreciate the ingenious construction of this story by means of gematria. It is a masterpiece—both beautiful and deeply significant. In figure 9.1, we see a circle inscribed in a square, and the circle's

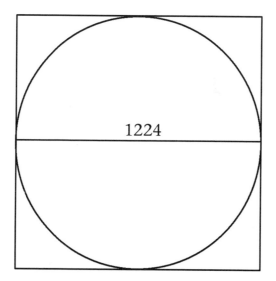

Figure 9.1. *The Holy City of the Fishes.*

diameter and the side of the square are both 1224. The circle is a symbol of perfection and can stand as an image of paradise—a garden enclosed. Since the purpose of the temple, in this case the Holy City, was to provide a template or pattern for the beneficial proportions reconciling opposing energies, the square surrounding the circle is an appropriate figure of the "sacred marriage" of masculine and feminine. Here it represents the nuptials of the New Jerusalem, the Holy City arrayed as a bride in the Book of Revelation. The number used to designate the Holy City as computed by John Michell is 1224, a highly significant number because it is the sacred sum of the Greek nominative plural *ιχθγες,* "fishes," and also for *το δικτυον,* "the net." Other important New Testament phrases Michell links to the New Jerusalem by means of this number 1224 include the Greek for "God's creation," "God's paradise," and "I am the Way."[10]

John Michell mentions other facts that are pertinent to our discussion of the traditional bride of Christ—the New Jerusalem. The number 1225 (1224 plus the *colel* of 1) is the sum of the phrase used by Plato in his *Timaeus,* "one whole of wholes" (*εν ολον ολων*), which designates the cosmos and embraces all its parts—the very epitome of wholeness.[11] The sum of all the numbers in sequence from 1 to 49 totals 1225, and 49 is 7^2, so 1225 is associated with "Wisdom" and things eternal and spiritual. How appropriate that the Church fathers in the early fourth century chose to celebrate the birthday of Christ at the midnight transition between the twenty-fourth and twenty-fifth day of the twelfth month of Rome's Julian calendar, thereby identifying Jesus Christ as "Lord of the Fishes," 1224, and of the entire cosmos, 1225. In the old Roman calendar that used March as the first month, December was the tenth (explaining the origin of its name). In 46 B.C. a decree by Julius Caesar established January as the first month, making December the twelfth throughout his empire. The date December 25 for the birth of Jesus was established by the middle of the fourth century, a half-century before the "numbers theology" of the Gnostics was brutally suppressed, forcing them to hide their library in jars and bury them in the Egyptian desert. Because of its proximity to the winter solstice marking the beginning of the sunlight's gradual increase, this date carries the symbolic significance of the "birth of the Sun/Son," but the esoteric meaning of Christmas is the "birth of the cosmic Lord of the New Age—the Fishes."

When we examine the number of the fishes we discover that the sum 1224 can be factored to 153 × 8. Remembering that there were exactly 153 fishes in the unbroken net (John 21) and our earlier discussion of the importance of the number eight in the New Testament, we pause to examine these significant symbolic numbers. We noted earlier that the Greek spelling for the name of Jesus was computed to be 888, denoting the rising sun or dawn of the New Age. The number eight was equated with regeneration and the new day or "new order," and the gematria of the Greek *Kyrios* (Lord) is 800. Origen and other Christian patriarchs and particularly Gnostic Christians often called Jesus the *ogdoad*, the "fullness of eights." So in the esoteric language of symbolic numbers, the 1224 diameter of our New Jerusalem is 8 × 153—the new day of the Fishes.

And we should not be surprised to learn that the number 153 itself also has immensely significant properties. The number can be factored into 17×3^2. Like the numbers 10, 666, and 1225, 153 is another so-called triangular number: if we calculate the sum of all the whole numbers from 1 to 17, the result is 153. So 17 and 153 have a significant relationship with each other. And 17 neatly illustrates the "new creation"—it is $4^2 + 1$. As nine is understood as a "trinity of threes," sixteen is a "quaternity of fours," reminiscent of the four corners of the earth and the square that symbolically represents Earth. Seen from all these various angles, the number seventeen, whose sum is eight, might be expressed as "the new creation" or "the new day on Earth" or perhaps even "the transformation of all earthly things."

The perfect six-petaled flower or star formed in the center of

Figure 9.2. *"The Seed of Life" mandala represents perfection.*

this mandala is the same image as the sixfold symbol for wholeness we discussed in earlier chapters, each petal having a length
of 306 (153 × 2), the measurement of the radius of each of the
equal seven circles. So, the number 153 is a basic measurement
necessary for the New Jerusalem, the city identified as the Bride
of the Lamb. And the wisdom number seven is beautifully contained in the image of the seven equal circles within the larger
outer circle of the mandala whose diameter is 1224—equated
with the "Fishes" of John's Gospel and by the addition of the *colel*
of 1 with the 1225 of Plato's cosmic unity—"one whole
of wholes."

But the correspondence that I found so illuminating was not
just that the diameter of the New Jerusalem was related to the
number for "Fishes" and that it was the symbolic equivalent of
"the new creation" and "a new heaven and a new earth" (Rev.
21:1). The correspondence that had me dancing in the street was
one that seems to have continuously eluded researchers for centuries. The number 153 is not only the number of fishes caught

in the net, nor is it merely a basic measurement of the Holy City. The number 153 is also by gematria the sum of the letters of η Μαγδαληνη, "the Magdalene."

This is monumental! The correlation of these numbers irrevocably links this beloved Mary with the mystical bride of Jesus, equating her with "transformation" and "the new creation" (17 × 3). She is the bearer of the archetype of bride, since 153—the number of the fishes in the net (John 21:11)—represents the chosen community or church of the new covenant. In the 1224, she is united with the bridegroom of her longing, represented by the number eight. The New Testament characterizes the Church as the bride "whom Christ loved so much he gave his life for her" (Eph. 5:25). From these simple calculations expressed in symbolic numbers, the Magdalene and the bride/Church are linked for all time in the gematria of the New Testament texts.

There is a further startling and profound meaning associated with the number 153: the number was universally recognized in Hellenistic times as denoting the $\emptyset$—the shape known to the Greeks as the matrix or the "measure of the fish." Greek geometers apparently used 153 as an abbreviation for the ratio 265/153, the value used by mathematicians to express √3.[12] It is the shape formed when the circumferences of two equal circles travel through one another's centers as in figure 9.3. The shared area of the overlapping circles forms a figure now known by its Latin name, the *vesica piscis* (literally, the "bladder of the fish"). If the horizontal axis of the *vesica piscis* is equal to 1, then the vertical axis is equal to √3. Not having a symbol for square root, the Greeks used whole-number ratios for irrational numbers such as √3, and thus labeled the vertical axis of the *vesica* 265 and the horizontal 153. The ratio 265/153 is an approximation of √3 that is accurate to five decimal places (1.73202). The Greek mathematician Archimedes (287–212 B.C.) describes this ratio in his treatise on circles, using 153 as a shorthand or abbreviation for this

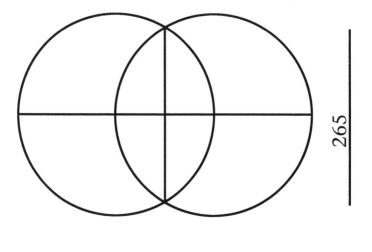

153

Figure 9.3. Intersecting circles form a vesica piscis
whose vertical and horizontal axes are in the ratio of
√3:1 or 265/153.

important **0** figure and for the √3, expressing it as commonplace
and not needing any further explanation.[13] The ratio designating
the *vesica piscis* was called simply "the 153."

The *vesica piscis* shape was extremely important in ancient
geometry, where it was recognized as the womb or matrix of all
other geometric forms. This highly significant symbol is shaped
like an almond, egg, or seed and was also associated with the
sacred feminine in the ancient world. The shape represented the
vulva and the "doorway of life"—epithets designed to reflect its
distinctly feminine connotations. In Goddess lore, it is called the
yoni, the feminine orifice. Its other name was "the Holy of
Holies"[14] with all its associations with the "bridal chamber." In
Western art, it is called the *mandorla* and often represents the
Holy Spirit in Christian symbolism. In many paintings and relief
sculptures Jesus is shown seated within this **0** shape.

Can it be merely accidental that the gematria for "the
Magdalene" is the number used in common parlance among

Greek mathematicians as a nickname for this same $\emptyset$ symbol from the ancient canon of sacred geometry? Hardly! While the name Maria found in the Gospels bears the gematria 152, only "the Magdalene" bears the exact gematria 153 associating her with the archetypal sacred feminine. Some New Testament exegetes saw her as the New Eve who, in partnership with Christ, the New Adam, came to restore the harmony that was lost in the Garden of Eden.

OUR TWO LADIES

Knowledge of gematria enhances immeasurably the esoteric meaning of the Christian Scriptures and forever establishes Mary the Magdalene as the human carrier or "incarnation" of the archetype of bride. She is the earthly representative of the Eternal Feminine—sacred cauldron of creativity and Holy Grail. Clearly, it was *this* Mary who was designated by the earliest creators of the New Testament doctrines to be the cosmic counterpart of Jesus, the Lord. The authors of the Gospels, the architects of the New Jerusalem, cannot have been oblivious to the numbers generated when they coined her epithet revealing the archetypal feminine. Together, she and Jesus represent the eternal bride and bridegroom whose sacred partnership—the hieros gamos—formed the cosmic center of the New Jerusalem, whose blueprint was the new mandala for the Piscean Age. Only in later generations was her character redefined: she was called prostitute, and her special mantle of honor was stripped away and bestowed upon the mother of Jesus as Queen of Heaven and Earth. But that does not alter the strong probability that the very earliest Christians who knew her best intended to designate the Magdalene as the Virgo counterpart of the Piscean Lord.

In the beginning, it was Mary Magdalene, the "Daughter of Zion," who was the carrier of *ekklesia,* the Church. She represented the penitent and redeemed community, the symbolic bride for whom Christ sacrificed his life. Early exegetes of the New Testament were in no doubt about this role of the Magdalene. It was she who was identified with the bride from the Canticles who sought her beloved at the tomb and was elated to be reunited with him. She was the "myrrhophore"—the bearer of perfumed ointment for the embalming of the sacrificed king. In Mark 14:8, Jesus acknowledged his anointing by the woman with the alabaster jar of precious nard: "She has anointed my body in preparation for burial." Magdalene's role was not confused with that of the mother of Jesus by those who wrote the Gospels; in the early Christian story, the roles of bride and mother were separate. In the Gospels they are named separately on lists that include the female companions of Jesus, but Magdalene is pre-eminent. They stood together at the foot of the cross, and in several Gospel accounts they apparently came together at dawn on Easter morning to the tomb of the crucified. Matthew's Gospel states that Mary Magdalene and the "other Mary" came to the tomb, while Mark calls the other Mary "the mother of James," an epithet that is repeated in Luke; in the Fourth Gospel, Mary Magdalene came alone to the garden sepulcher where she encountered the risen Lord.

The exaltation of the Virgin Mary as *theotokos*—"the Mother of God"—from the fifth century onward through fifteen millennia of Western civilization has provided us with an ideal feminine, a tender and compassionate mother set high on a pedestal, a beautiful queen and pure vision of chaste maidenhood. It was this vision of Mary as Queen that Pope John Paul II wished to see crowned in heaven as co-redemptrix with Jesus at the dawn of Christianity's third millennium. But this idea is not in keeping with Scripture. Beautiful as this eternal mother is, the representation of the eternal feminine as Virgin Mother does not provide us with a "partnership" paradigm—the model for life on planet Earth—as does the "sacred marriage" of Jesus and his true bride. Perhaps it is time to consider restoring the ancient paradigm of the hieros gamos in the temples of our minds and hearts—"on Earth as it is in heaven."

I do not for a moment imagine the Blessed Virgin Mary and Mary Magdalene as rival goddesses, jealous of their individual preeminence and squabbling over their prerogatives as did the female deities of the Greek pantheon. I envision the two Mariams first as two fully human women, a mother and her daughter-in-law, both deeply devoted to Jesus and to one another. I see them as two women who suffered together at the foot of the cross, each a source of comfort and strength to the other in their mutual sorrow. And I see them mutually supportive and entirely devoted to each other and to Jesus. Surely the Virgin Mary would in no way be demoted if her beloved daughter-in-law were finally and properly acknowledged as the bride of Jesus.

Prayers of the *anawim* will still and forever be addressed to the mother of Jesus, just as they have been in the past. She will continue to be honored and blessed as the vessel chosen to be the mother of the Messiah. But that does not mean that we should not also honor his beloved, so long neglected in our human psyche. By reclaiming the lost bride—the feminine complement of Christ—to the Christian mythology we would repair the broken mandala of the sacred marriage.

We await the ecstatic celebration—"the nuptials of the Lamb"—of Jesus the Christos and his archetypal bride, the Magdalene, who represents the enlightened and redeemed community arrayed in splendor on her wedding day:

> And I beheld the Holy City, a New Jerusalem
> coming down out of heaven from God,
> prepared as a bride adorned for her husband.
> I heard a loud voice from the throne saying,
> "Behold, God's dwelling is with the human race."
>
> REVELATION 21:2–3

This passage is the culmination of the ancient prophecy found in the prophetic Book of Isaiah, the nuptials of the bride—representing her entire people—united with her eternal bridegroom:

> *For Zion's sake I shall not be silent*
> *until her vindication shines forth like the dawn . . .*
> *No longer shall you be called "forsaken,"*
> *and your lands "desolate,"*
> *but you shall be called "beloved,"*
> *and your lands "espoused."*
>
> ISAIAH 62:1, 4

The prophesied nuptials of the Lamb and his Holy Bride will cause streams of living water to flow from the throne of God for the healing of the nations, causing the desert to bloom at last!

EROS DENIED

The preeminent institution of Western civilization most firmly entrenched in the patriarchal, hierarchical model is the Roman Catholic Church. The recent erosion of the credibility of the Catholic hierarchy has been painfully obvious. Allegations against pedophile priests and continuous attempts of the prelates to cover up the escalating number of such reports in order to prevent scandal have rocked Roman Catholic parishes around the world. I believe sexual abuse within the Church stems from a tragic design flaw in the institution whose "fathers" deliberately dissociate themselves from the feminine.

As we have discussed, the model for hieros gamos—the sacred union of the Christ couple—was broken at the dawn of Christianity. The subsequent adulation of the male power principle enthroned in heaven and on earth inevitably created a caste of privileged priests who have refused to share power with women and to become integrated with the feminine through marriage. Theirs is allegedly a "higher" calling, characterized by denial of the flesh and devotion to intellectual pursuits and spiritual practice. Almost three quarters of the canonized saints of the Roman Catholic Church are celibate men. The denial of sexuality enforced through the practice of celibacy often results in these individuals being sadly out of touch with the cycles of the feminine, the dark earth, the body wisdom, the passionate emotion, and the deep intuition frequently awakened through intimate relationship with the feminine, including sensual experience. Their vows of celibacy result in Eros denied, extending into all levels of human relationships: physical, emotional, intellectual, and spiritual. The sad consequences of Eros denied can be seen in the broken lives of priests who engaged in wrongful sexual activity as well as those of the victims of their abuses of power and trust.

Why did the Roman Catholic Church insist on requiring a vow of life-long celibacy from those who wished to be priests? At its inception, leaders of the church were married men. Peter had a mother-in-law, and Paul states that the brothers of Jesus and the other apostles travel with their "sister-brides." (1 Cor. 9:4). The model among the earliest Christians was gender equality and shared leadership, based, I believe, on the example provided by Mary Magdalene as an important leader in the community. Uta Ranke-Heinemann *(Eunuchs for the Kingdom of Heaven)* and Karen Jo Torjenson *(When Women Were Priests)* have written fascinating histories of the role of women in the Church. Recent research by Roman Catholic theologian and archaeologist Dorothy Irvin provides clear pictorial evidence of women dressed in priestly vestments and epithets describing their leadership roles, where some were acknowledged as *episcopa,* "bishops." Women were marginalized after 494 when the ordination of women into leadership roles was banned in a decree from Pope Gelasius.

Meanwhile, during earliest Christian tradition, priests had been allowed to marry. The movement to deny them this option intensified near the end of the 11th century, culminating when Pope Urban II ruled in 1095 that, henceforth, those seeking ordination could not be married. A later edict issued in 1139 by Pope Innocent II required married priests to abandon their wives and families. Did the Pope and his advisors somehow forget the word of God spoken in the book of Genesis: "It is not good for the man to be alone. I will make a partner for him" (Gen. 2: 18)? Their publicly stated reason for adopting the new prerequisite for priesthood was to insure that Church property would not be inherited by children of priests but would remain in the hands of the hierarchy. However, underlying the decision of the papacy was the belief that, in order to consolidate the power of the Church, it was necessary to wrest the priests from the influence of their wives. This was noted in a public declaration by Pope Innocent II stating that the Church could not escape from the clutches of the laity unless priests first escaped the clutches of their wives.

Mandatory celibacy, enforced after 1139, appears to have concretized the erroneous assumption that Jesus was celibate. In light of the gematria of the "grain of mustard seed" and the partnership of the "Fishes" confirming the sacred marriage at the heart of the Christian mythology, this tradition needs to be reassessed. The original model—the partnership paradigm—was distorted by later teachings and eventually became thoroughly established in the dogmas, traditions, and doctrines of the Vatican Magesterium in Rome, which support the patriarchal institution, par excellence, still existing in modern times. In addition to the mandatory celibacy of priests, other important issues that are closely related to the denial of the "Sacred Feminine" include gender equality and acceptance of women priests, the ban on birth control, and the whole issue of clerical prestige and authority, privilege and power. Balance will only be restored to the contemporary Church when full gender equality is embraced: the demand for celibacy lifted, women ordained, and Mary the "Beloved" is restored to her archetypal Bridegroom in Sacred Union.

> "In the cities ...shall yet be heard
> the cry of joy, the cry of gladness,
> the voice of the bridegroom,
> the voice of the bride."
>
> JER. 33: 10B-11A

Ave Millennium! 99

NOTES

Chapter 1

1. Harold Bayley, *The Lost Language of Symbolism* (1912; reprint,Totowa, N.J.: Rowman & Littlefield, 1974).
2. Alexander Cruden, *Cruden's Unabridged Concordance* (Grand Rapids, Mich.: Baker Book House, 1973), 582.
3. Riane Eisler, *The Chalice and the Blade* (San Francisco: Harper & Row, 1988), 72.
4. Tons Brunés, *The Secrets of Ancient Geometry—and Its Use*, trans. Charles M. Napier (Copenhagen: Rhodos, 1967), 1:248–49.
5. John Michell, *The Dimensions of Paradise: The Proportions and Symbolic Numbers of Ancient Cosmology* (1988; reprint, San Francisco: Harper & Row, 1990), 193.
6. Merlin Stone, *When God Was a Woman* (New York: The Dial Press, 1976), 67.
7. Bayley, *Lost Language of Symbolism*, 2:161.

Chapter 2

1. Brunés, *Secrets of Ancient Geometry*, 1:47–48.
2. Ibid., 1:46.
3. John Michell, *The City of Revelation: On the Proportions and Symbolic Numbers of the Cosmic Temple* (1971; reprint, New York: David McKay Company, 1972), 7.
4. See Fred Gettings, *The Secret Zodiac* (London: Routledge & Kegan Paul, 1987). This fascinating study discusses the thirteenth-century cathedral of San Miniato. Louis Charpentier reveals principles of sacred geometry

in the design of Chartres Cathedral in *Mysteries of Chartres Cathedral*, trans. Ronald Fraser and Janette Jackson (Northamptonshire: Thorsons, 1972). Henry Lincoln gives further examples of chapels built on special alignments in *The Holy Place* (New York: Arcade Publishing, 1991).

5. See Charpentier, *Mysteries of Chartres Cathedral*, chap. 13, "The Mystery of the Plan," 109–17, for the sevenfold basis of the con-struction of Notre Dame de Chartres.

6. Brunés, *Secrets of Ancient Geometry*, 1:147–76.

7. Herbert Silberer, *Hidden Symbolism of Alchemy and the Occult Arts* (1917; reprint New York: Dover Publications, 1971), 399.

CHAPTER 3

1. Michell, *Dimensions of Paradise*. This book includes new information not included in his earlier book on the ancient canon of sym-bolic numbers, *The City of Revelation*.

2. Mitchell, *Dimensions of Paradise*, 173.

3. Jerry Lucas and Del Washburn, *Theomatics: God's Best Kept Secret Revealed* (New York: Stein and Day, 1977), 17. Lucas and Washburn use a *colel* (discrepancy factor) of ± 2 for their calculations, which makes cor-respondences easier to achieve than with the more demanding ± 1 of classical Greek and Hebrew usage.

4. David Fideler, *Jesus Christ, Sun of God* (Wheaton, Ill.: Quest Books, 1993), 219.

5. Lucas and Washburn, *Theomatics*, 203–45. Washburn and Lucas devote their chapter 8 to the clusters associated with the "144 thou-sands" in the New Jerusalem.

CHAPTER 4

1. Michell, *Dimensions of Paradise*, 107.

2. Two of the most valuable resources for establishing the widespread use of gematria in the New Testament are John Michell's *The City of Revelation* and *The Dimensions of Paradise*. Further resources are David Fideler, *Jesus Christ, Sun of God*, and Lucas and Washburn, *Theomatics*.

3. Michell, *Dimensions of Paradise*, 185–93.

4. Ibid., 193–95, provides a complete list of New Testament phrases adding up to 1746, ± 1.

5. Jean-Yves Leloupe, *The Gospel of Mary Magdalene*, trans. Joseph Rowe (Rochester, Vt.: Bear & Company, 2002), 13, n. 17 (comment of translator). Although it is currently popular believe that Jesus was a carpenter who

spoke only Aramaic, scholars deem it more likely that he also understood and spoke Koiné.

6. Michell, *Dimensions of Paradise,* 29–33.
7. Hippolytus of Rome (c. 170–235) in his commentary on the Song of
   Songs equates the dark Shulamite bride with Mary Magdalene seeking
   her beloved in the garden.
8. Michell, *Dimensions of Paradise,* 9–10.
9. Ibid., 32–34 (figures 6 and 7) and 172–73.

Chapter 5

1. This argument about the context of the "eunuchs for the kingdom of
   heaven" is explained by Dr. William E. Phipps, *Was Jesus Married?* (New
   York: Harper & Row, 1970), 79–86.
2. Robert Funk et al., *The Five Gospels* (New York: Macmillan, 1993), 30–31.
3. Lucas and Washburn, *Theomatics,* ch. 6, 138–76.
4. Ibid.
5. James Carroll, *The Sword of Constantine* (New York: Houghton-Mifflin,
   2001). This book discusses the history of enmity between Christianity
   and Judaism beginning with its roots in the Christian Scriptures, especially certain anti-Semitic passages found in the Gospel of John.

Chapter 6

1. Scripture scholars hypothesize that the Gospel authors used a lost written source of the sayings of Jesus known as "Q" (German Quelle) in
   compiling their written versions of the ministry of Jesus.
2. See Raymond Brown, *The Community of the Beloved Disciple* (New York:
   Paulist Press, 1979), for a thorough discussion of various Christologies
   among early Christian communities.
3. Ibid.

Chapter 7

1. See Elisabeth Schüssler Fiorenza, *The Book of Revelation: Justice and
   Judgment* (Philadelphia: Fortress Press, 1984), for amplification of this
   general theme.
2. Michell, *Dimensions of Paradise,* 10.
3. Ibid., 60.
4. Ibid., 190.
5. Clusters and cognates of 111 are discussed in Lucas and Washburn,
   Theomatics, ch. 3, 49–88.

6. Clusters of 666's are found in Lucas and Washburn, *Theomatics*, ch. 7, 177–202.

7. Leloupe, *The Gospel of Mary Magdalene*, 161. Leloupe paraphrases Karl Graf von Dürkheim concerning the wedding that must take place within the human person between two hemispheres of the brain, and on a universal and planetary level between the archetypes of "Orient" and "Occident."

8. Ibid., 168–69. Leloupe sees Mary Magdalene as the Holy Bride/Jerusalem. Also: "Miriam (the Magdalene) is the woman of Desire, which includes all desires, from those of the flesh to those of the highest reaches of soul, mind, and spirit. She is the holy bride who unites with her Beloved to say to all: 'Come!'" (167).

9. Associated clusters of the "144 thousands" are found in Lucas and Washburn, *Theomatics*, ch.8, 203–45.

10. Michell, *Dimensions of Paradise*, 197.

11. See Margaret Starbird, *The Woman with the Alabaster Jar* (Santa Fe: Bear & Company, 1993).

CHAPTER 8

1. Michell, *Dimensions of Paradise*, 195–98. This theory is discussed also by Carl G. Jung in *Aion* (Princeton, N.J.: Princeton University Press, 1968).

2. Fideler, *Jesus Christ, Sun of God*, 169.

3. F. Edward Hulme, *Symbolism in Christian Art* (1891; reprint, Detroit: Gale Research Co., 1969), 203.

4. See Michell, *Dimensions of Paradise*, 170–98, for in-depth summary of this thesis.

5. For discussion of political considerations on the authors of the canonical Gospels, see S. G. F. Brandon, *Jesus and the Zealots* (New York: Charles Scribner's Sons, 1967). Also see Carroll, *The Sword of Constantine*.

6. See Brown, *Community of the Beloved Disciple*, for research comparing various levels of Christology among first-century Christians.

CHAPTER 9

1. Susan Haskins, *Mary Magdalene, Myth and Metaphor* (1993; reprint, New York: Harcourt Brace, 1993) 48.

2. Michell, *Dimensions of Paradise*, 197.

3. See Morton Smith, *The Secret Gospel* (New York: Harper & Row, 1973), 50–51. In the Secret Gospel of Mark, Mary of Bethany prostrates herself before Jesus and the disciples rebuke her, presumably for breaking her

shiva without her husband's permission. In John's Gospel, the passage is changed: Mary waits in the house until Martha tells her that Jesus is asking for her.

4. French legends of the Sangraal (Holy Grail) say that Mary Magdalene brought the Holy Grail to France in A.D. 42, seeking political exile as a refugee from persecution suffered in Jerusalem. When the word *sangraal* is divided after the *g* (rather than the *n*) the two words resulting mean "blood royal" in Old French. From this, it is a short step to the "heresy" of the Holy Grail, which claims that a child of the union of Jesus and Mary Magdalene survived. For this theory about the Sangraal, see Michael Baigent, Henry Lincoln, and Richard Leigh, *Holy Blood, Holy Grail* (New York: Dell, 1983), and Starbird, *The Woman with the Alabaster Jar.*

5. James Robinson, ed., "The Gospel of Philip," in *The Nag Hammadi Library: In English* (San Francisco: Harper & Row, 1981), 138.

6. Marvin H. Pope, *Song of Songs,* Anchor Bible Series (Garden City, N.Y.: Doubleday, 1983), 19. See also Samuel N. Kramer, *The Sacred Marriage Rite* (Bloomington: Indiana University Press, 1969) 85–105.

7. Kramer, *Sacred Marriage Rite,* 133.

8. Michell, *Dimensions of Paradise,* 174–78.

9. Fideler, *Jesus Christ, Sun of God,* 291–308.

10. Michell, *Dimensions of Paradise,* 174.

11. Ibid.

12. Fideler, *Jesus Christ, Sun of God,* 307.

13. Ibid.

14. See Jonathan Hale, *The Old Way of Seeing* (Boston: Houghton Mifflin, 1994), 76–85, for detailed discussion of the *vesica piscis* in art and symbolism. For the relationship of the *vesica piscis* with Mary Magdalene and the gematria of her name, see Margaret Starbird, *The Goddess in the Gospels* (Santa Fe: Bear & Company, 1998), 159–60.

GLOSSARY

Apocalypse of John (also "Book of Revelation")

Final book of the New Testament, (written c.95–100 A.D.). Prophetic Greek text describes the wrath of God poured out and final reconciliation with the nuptials of the Lamb and his Bride, the Holy City/Church.

Apocalyptic

Belief that the world will be destroyed by direct intervention by God and that a new and better world will be put in place where peace and justice will be established.

Aramaic

Native language related to Hebrew spoken by Semitic peoples of Palestine during the time of Jesus.

Archetype

Model or pattern of behavior that is universally recognized and accepted: Warrior, Sage, Lover, Divine Child.

Archimedes

Greek philosopher/mathematician. Third century B.C.

Athene

Greek Goddess of Wisdom, patroness of Athens.

Canon

Authoritative books accepted as "Scripture."

Canon of Sacred Number

Codified values of dimensions and relationships of sun, moon, and planets derived by Greek philosopher Pythagoras and his school to reflect the order and harmony of the universe.

Christology

Study of the true role and nature of Jesus Christ in an attempt to reconcile the human and the divine articulated in the doctrine of the Incarnation.

Codex

A stack of written sheets stacked and bound together; replaced the use of parchment scrolls in first century.

Colel

Value of ±1 (poetic license) used in determining correspondences by gematria.

Coptic

Egyptian language in early centuries of Christianity, in which Gnostic Gospels found at Nag Hammadi were written.

Cosmology

Worldview of the universe based on combination of science and mythology.

Docetism

Belief that Jesus only appeared to be human but was actually pure spirit.

Druid's cord

Measuring line with twelve knots at equal intervals forming thirteen equal segments used in building to form a Pythagorean triangle (right triangle with sides of 3, 4, and 5 units) and an isosceles triangle (sides of 4, 4, and 5 units).

Ebionites

Early Christians linked to the conservative Jewish community in Jerusalem who remained loyal to the Torah and the Temple.

Gematria

Literary device involving use of the numerical values of Hebrew and Greek letters to calculate sums reflecting significant symbolic numbers and proportions codified in the sacred canon of the Pythagoreans.

Gnostic Gospels

Gospels of Philip, Thomas, Peter, and Mary among others written in Coptic and hidden with other Gnostic texts in earthen jars during period of persecution by orthodox Christians (c. 400).

Gnosticism

Individualistic religion based on direct revelation rather than institutionalized liturgies and prayers.

Gospels

Sacred texts proclaim the "Good News" of Jesus and his ministry, death, and resurrection. There are four canonical Gospels—Matthew, Mark, Luke, John—and numerous other apocryphal and Gnostic Gospels.

h Magdalhnh

The Greek epithet of Mary Magdalene in the Christian Gospels.

Hebrew Bible

Sacred texts of Judaism: forty-six books including the Torah (Pentateuch), history books, Psalms, writings of prophets, Wisdom books, Song of Songs.

Ichthys

"Fish" abbreviated from the intials of the Greek phrase "Jesus Christ, Son of God, Savior." Jesus was called the "Fish" by several early Church Fathers.

Jerusalem

Holy City of David located in Israel, symbolic center of the universe and symbolic "Bride" of God.

Koiné Greek

Lingua franca spoken and written in the eastern Mediterranean lands of the Roman Empire in the Near East. The language in which the texts of the New Testament were written.

***Magdala* (also *Migdol*)**

Hebrew word meaning "stronghold," "citadel," "watchtower." Town in Galilee now known as Magdala did not exist at the time of Jesus.

Mithraism

Religion based on the cult of Mithras having many similarities to Christianity popular among Romans.

Mystery religions

Cults emphasizing personal transformation and salvation through identification with Dionysus, Demeter or Isis/Osiris, Orpheus, and other deities. Many Jews believed that Christianity was a mystery cult.

Nag Hammadi codices

Sacred texts of Gnostic Christians hidden during persecutions by orthodox Christians in about 400 and discovered in 1945.

Origen

Christian patriarch (c. 185–254).

Parable

Brief story centered on metaphor taken from common life or nature used to teach truth by analogy. Many teachings of Jesus were expressed in parables.

Pericopes

Portions or segments of stories about Jesus that probably circulated independently in an oral tradition and were eventually included in various Gospels.

Pisces

"Fishes," the constellation of the zodiac rising at the time of the birth of Jesus; Sign of the New Age that began at the beginning of the current era.

Plato

Greek philosopher and initiate into the mysteries of Pythagorean School and wisdom of Egyptian and Persian priests.

Pythagorean School

Custodians of the secrets of sacred geometry, symbolic number, and cosmology/science based on teachings of Pythagoras, 580–500 B.C.

Sacred geometry

Mathematical values derived from actual measurements of the planets, sun, and moon codified into certain numbers and proportions that reflected the order of the created universe.

Sirach

Book of collected teachings of Jesus ben Sira (c. 200–174); apocryphal book of Old Testament is called Sirach or Ecclesiasticus.

Sophia

Wisdom identified as a female figure, honored as the "Immaculate Mirror" of God's Energy and "Spouse of the Lord" by Gnostic and Greek Christians. She is further identified with the Holy Spirit and with the Jewish Shekhinah, "the emanation of the Glory of God," and the "sacred feminine consciousness."

Synoptic Gospels

Greek word meaning "having the same view." Gospels of Matthew, Mark, and Luke have so many similarities of form and content that they appear to have been derived from the same sources.

Temple of Solomon

Temple built during King Solomon's reign on the Temple Mount in Jerusalem, destroyed in 586 B.C. The "Second Temple" was built on the same site in 516 and was later renovated and rebuilt by King Herod (reigned 37–4).

Tetractys

The first ten values (1–10) displayed in four rows of dots that form a triangle representing the prime building block of the universe.

Torah

The Law of Israel, contained in the first five books of the Hebrew Bible, also called the Pentateuch.

Vesica Piscis ◊

The "measure" or "matrix of the fish" identified with the feminine orifice, "gateway of life." The symbol is the "mother of all geometry" is formed when two circles intersect and overlap. Represents the "Grail" or "Chalice," also "Sacred Cauldron of Creativity."

Yin/Yang ☯

Symbol represening Oriental philosophy of masculine/feminine energies as interrelated complementary opposites.

Zodiac

Imaginary belt composed of twelve constellations (represented by familiar astrological signs) through which the earth passes in order during a yearly cycle.

CHRONOLOGY

B.C.

7000–3000	Neolithic period; god-goddess fertility cults celebrated
c. 3100	Newgrange passage tomb built in Ireland
2800–2400	Kingdom of Sumer
2700–2200	Pyramids built in Egypt
2000–1500	Megalithic monuments, Stonehenge built in England
1800–1600	Age of Jewish Patriarchs: Abraham, Isaac, Jacob, Joseph, and his eleven brothers
c. 1275–1250	Moses leads the Children of Israel out of Egypt; receives the Ten Commandments. Joshua conquers Canaan—"The Holy Land"
c. 1020–1002	King Saul rules Israel
c. 1002–962	King David rules Israel
c. 962–922	King Solomon rules; builds the First Temple in Jerusalem
727–707	Sargon II, ruler of Babylon, first uses gematria
586	Nebuchadnezzar's armies conquer Jerusalem, burn the Temple
586–539	Jewish people enslaved in Babylon
580–500	Pythagoras, Greek philosopher, develops canon of symbolic number
516	Jewish people return to Jerusalem, rebuild the Temple

Please send us this card to receive our latest catalog.

☐ Check here if you would like to receive our catalog via e-mail.

E-mail address _____

Name _____ Company _____

Address _____

City _____ State _____ Zip _____ Country _____

Please check the following area(s) of interest to you:

☐ Health   ☐ Self-help   ☐ Science/Nature ☐ Shamanism
☐ Ancient Mysteries ☐ New Age/Spirituality ☐ Ethnobotany   ☐ Martial Arts
☐ Spanish Language ☐ Sexuality/Tantra   ☐ Children   ☐ Teen

Order at 1-800-246-8648 • Fax (802) 767-3726
E-mail: orders@InnerTraditions.com • Web site: www.InnerTraditions.com

INNER TRADITIONS

BEAR & CO.

BEAR CUB BOOKS

HEALING·ARTS·PRESS

DESTINY BOOKS

ParkStreet Press

BINDU BOOKS

Inner Traditions • Bear & Company

P.O. Box 388
Rochester, VT 05767-0388
U.S.A.

Affix
Postage
Stamp
Here

428–348	Plato, initiate into secrets of priests and philosophers/mathematicians
384–322	Aristotle, Greek scientist and philosopher of reason
356–323	Alexander the Great conquers an empire that includes India, Egypt
333–63	Greek hegemony over Palestine, Egypt, and Near East. Gematria first used in Hebrew during this period of Greek influence
c. 300	Euclid, Greek mathematician and geometer
287–212	Archimedes, Greek mathematician
33	Romans conquer Greek Empire. Beginning of Roman hegemony in Near East
44	Assassination of Julius Caesar
37–4	Reign of Herod the Great in Judea; Temple rebuilt on a grand scale
c 7–4	Birth of Jesus

A.D.

c. 28–29	Likely date of ministry of Jesus in Judea and Galilee
c. 36–38	Conversion of Saul/Paul on the road to Damascus
45–62	Paul's missionary journeys; Epistles to various communities
62–65	Book of Acts written, probably by Luke the Evangelist; Nero burns Rome; martyrdom of Peter and Paul in Rome
66–70	Jewish revolt against Rome; Herod's Temple destroyed
c. 70–71	Gospel of Mark written
73	Fall of the last Jewish stronghold at Masada
c. 80–85	Gospel of Matthew
c. 85	Gospel of Luke
c. 90–95	Gospel of John
c. 95–100	Apocalypse of John (Book of Revelation) written

100–300	Gnostic Gospels written
130–200	Irenaeus of Lyons, author of *Against Heresies,* castigats Gnostics
170–235	Hippolytus of Rome, New Testament exegete; Song of Songs commentary
185–254	Origen
340–420	Jerome translates Greek Scriptures into Latin, obscuring gematria
c. 400	Gnostic Gospels hidden in earthen jars near Nag Hammadi
354–430	Saint Augustine, Bishop of Hippo
500	Rome falls to barbarian armies, Empire disintegrates
591	In a homily Pope Gregory the Great declares Mary Magdalene to be identified with the sister of Lazarus who anointed Jesus and the "sinner" in Luke's Gospel
550–700	Muslim armies sweep across Near East and Africa, conquer Spain
500–1000	Dark Ages in Europe. Barbarian hordes and Viking raids threaten civilization; rise of monastic orders preserves scholarship/culture
732	Defeat of Moors' invasion at Battle of Tours saves Christian Europe
800	Charlemagne crowned Holy Roman Emperor by Pope in Rome
1098–1099	First Crusade of Europeans conquers Jerusalem from Saracens
1117	Order of the Poor Knights of the Temple of Solomon established
1130–1250	Chartres, Rheims, Amiens, and other cathedrals of Our Lady built on pattern of constellation Virgo employing principles of sacred geometry
1209–1240	Albigensian Crusade in southern France
1237	Inquisition established to eradicate heresies

1291	Crusaders expelled from the Near East
1307	Knights of the Temple liquidated, members imprisoned and martyred
1492	Columbus discovers the Americas
1500	End of Middle Ages/Beginning of Renaissance

BIBLIOGRAPHY

Baigent, Michael, Richard Leigh, and Henry Lincoln. *Holy Blood, Holy Grail.* New York: Dell Publishing Co., 1983.

Bayley, Harold. *The Lost Language of Symbolism.* 1912. Reprint, Totowa, N.J.: Rowman & Littlefield, 1974.

Brandon, S. G. F. *Jesus and the Zealots.* New York: Charles Scribner's Sons, 1967.

Brown, Raymond E. *The Community of the Beloved Disciple.* New York: Paulist Press, 1979.

————, ed. *The Jerome Biblical Commentary.* Englewood Cliffs, N.J.: Prentice Hall, 1968.

Brunés, Tons. *The Secrets of Ancient Geometry—and Its Use.* Trans. Charles M. Napier. Copenhagen: Rhodos, 1967.

Carroll, James. *The Sword of Constantine.* New York: Houghton-Mifflin, 2001.

Cartlidge, David R., and David L. Dungan, eds. *Documents for Study of the Gospels.* Philadelphia: Fortress Press, 1980.

Charpentier, Louis. *The Mysteries of Chartres Cathedral.* Trans. Ronald Fraser and Janette Jackson. Northamptonshire: Thorson's, 1972.

Collins, John J. *The Apocalyptic Imagination.* 1987. Reprint, Grand Rapids, Mich.: Eerdmans Publishing Co., 1998.

Cruden, Alexander. *Cruden's Unabridged Concordance.* Grand Rapids, Mich.: Baker Book House, 1973.

Daniélou, Jean. *The Dead Sea Scrolls and Primitive Christianity.* Trans. Salvator Attanasio. New York: New American Library, 1962.

Eisler, Riane. *The Chalice and the Blade.* San Francisco: Harper & Row, 1988.

Fideler, David. *Jesus Christ, Sun of God*. Wheaton, Ill.: Quest Books, 1993.

Fiorenza, Elisabeth Schüssler. *The Book of Revelation: Justice and Judgment*. Philadelphia: Fortress Press, 1984.

Franz, Marie-Louise von. *Alchemy*. Toronto: Inner City Books, 1980.

Gettings, Fred. *The Secret Zodiac*. London: Routledge & Kegan Paul, 1987.

Halliday, William R. *The Pagan Background of Early Christianity*. New York: Cooper Square Publishers, 1970.

Hansen, Paul D. *Visionaries and Their Apocalypses*. Philadelphia: Fortress Press, 1983.

Haskins, Susan. *Mary Magdalene, Myth and Metaphor*. New York: Harcourt Brace, 1993.

Hulme, F. Edward. *Symbolism in Christian Art*. 1891. Reprint, Detroit: Gale Research Co., 1969.

Inman, Thomas. *Ancient Pagan and Modern Christian Symbolism*. 1884. Reprint, Williamstown, Mass.: Corner House Publishers, 1978.

Jenkins, Ferrell. *The Old Testament in the Book of Revelation*. Grand Rapids, Mich.: Baker Book House, 1972.

Kelly, J. N. D. *Early Christian Creeds*. New York: David McKay, 1972.

Kramer, Samuel N. *The Sacred Marriage Rite*. Bloomington: Indiana University Press, 1969.

Laws, Sophie. *In the Light of the Lamb*. Wilmington, Del.: Glazier, Inc., 1988.

Leloupe, Jean-Yves. *The Gospel of Mary Magdalene*. Trans. Joseph Rowe. Rochester, Vt.: Bear&Company, 2002.

Lincoln, Henry. *The Holy Place*. New York: Arcade Publishing, 1991.

Lucas, Jerry and Del Washburn. *Theomatics: God's Best Kept Secret Revealed*. New York: Stein and Day, 1977.

Michell, John. *The City of Revelation*. 1971. Reprint, New York: David McKay, 1972.

———. *The Dimensions of Paradise*. 1988. Reprint, San Francisco: Harper & Row, 1990.

Patai, Raphael. *The Hebrew Goddess*. Hoboken, N.J.: KTAV Publishing House, 1967.

Phipps, William E. *Was Jesus Married?* New York: Harper & Row, 1970.

———. *The Sexuality of Jesus*. New York: Harper & Row, 1973.

Pilch, John J. *What Are They Saying about the Book of Revelation?* New York: Paulist Press, 1978.

Pope, Marvin H. *Song of Songs*. Anchor Bible Series. Garden City, N.Y.: Doubleday, 1983.

Qualls-Corbett, Nancy. *The Sacred Prostitute*. Toronto: Inner City Books, 1988.

Ranke-Heinemann, Uta. *Eunuchs for the Kingdom of Heaven: Women, Sexuality and the Catholic Church*. Trans. Peter Heinegg. New York: Doubleday, 1990.

Ringgren, Helmar. *The Faith of Qumran*. Trans. Emilie T. Sander. Philadelphia: Fortress Press, 1963.

———. *Religions of the Ancient Near East*. Trans. John Sturdy. Philadelphia: Westminster Press, 1973.

Robinson, James M., ed. *The Nag Hammadi Library: In English*. San Francisco: Harper & Row, 1981.

Russell, D. S. *The Method and Message of Jewish Apocalyptic*. Philadelphia: Westminster Press, 1964.

Schick, Edwin A. *Revelation, the Last Book of the Bible*. Philadelphia: Fortress Press, 1977.

Schonfield, Hugh. *The Pentecost Revolution*. Dorset, England: Element Books, 1985.

Silberer, Herbert. *Hidden Symbolism of Alchemy and the Occult Arts*. 1917. Reprint, New York: Dover Publications, 1971.

Sparks, H. F. D., ed. *The Apocryphal Old Testament*. New York: Oxford University Press, 1984.

Starbird, Margaret. *The Goddess in the Gospels: Reclaiming the Sacred Feminine*. Santa Fe: Bear & Company, 1998.

———. *The Woman with the Alabaster Jar: Mary Magdalen and the Holy Grail*. Santa Fe: Bear & Company, 1993.

Stone, Merlin. *When God Was a Woman*. New York: The Dial Press, 1976.

Vermes, G. *The Dead Sea Scrolls in English*. New York: Penguin Books, 1987.

BIBLES

The Bible: New International Version. New York: The American Bible Society, 1978.

Joseph New Catholic Edition of the Holy Bible. New York: Catholic Book Publishing Co., 1963.

The NKJV Greek English Interlinear New Testament. Trans. Arthur L. Farstad, Zane C. Hodges, C. Michael Moss, Robert E. Picirilli, Wilbur N. Pickering. Nashville: Thomas Nelson Publishers, 1994.

INDEX